TESTIMONIALS

"Mooji's words are irrefutable pointers to That which is true in us, That which cannot die."

– *Mirabai Yaniv*

"What grace has showered upon us to hear the utterances of God himself fall from our most holiest father's lips. As we bathe in our Master's grace-filled words, the tides of his wisdom rise up within us, washing away all that is untrue. Each one of these quotes is a gateway into the very heart of Moojiji's teachings. Sink deeply into any one of them and drown in the emptiness of Being.
I love you Guruji."

– *Lakshmi Paice*

"Mooji's quotes are a powerful satsang tool. They are satsang questions being answered without being asked. It doesn't matter the form they take— book, website, Facebook or through a friend—if they are in front of your eyes, it is because God is answering you directly. This is evidence that Mooji is always with you."

– *Ishwari Reyes*

"Sri Mooji's grace cannot be mistaken. We are infinitely privileged to be reading the words from the Buddha in this modern age. And with Sri Moojiji's confidence that everyone has to get this timeless Truth, my wish is that this message will touch you as well as so many others around the world so that the world can rest in its effortless state as peace, harmony and unending contentment."

– *Rose Wallrock*

"Sri Mooji and his pointings are one. He speaks our heart's true voice urging us to come home. Though seemingly coming from outside, his satsang shows that there is no inside and outside, all is here, all is one. He is a holy man and a true master who has the power to raise us up to our own holiness. I love him endlessly."

– *Roos Le Roux*

"Mooji is a living Christ, a living Buddha, a living Krishna, here with us on earth today. He is the immortal one that lives inside our own heart and awakens the Truth in those whose lives call them to discover their timeless, undying nature."

– *Mahima Anderson*

"Mooji is no longer outside of me. Since finding his pointing inside my being, I see his eyes in everyone. He is the very source of life itself. As he took me into his most compassionate, loving heart, I too experience this universal love that consumes the slightest particle of doubt and leaves one with the freshness of freedom."

– *Shivali Haydvogel*

White Fire

SPIRITUAL INSIGHTS AND TEACHINGS OF ADVAITA ZEN MASTER MOOJI

Mooji

NON-DUALITY PRESS
An Imprint of New Harbinger Publications

WHITE FIRE

Original English version first published in 2014 by

Mooji Media Publications

A trade name of Mooji Media Ltd., UK

Distributed in Canada by Raincoast Books

Copyright © 2014 by Mooji Media Ltd.
Non-Duality Press
An imprint of New Harbinger Publications
5674 Shattuck Avenue
Oakland, CA 94609

Edited by Gayatri, Sumantra, and Zenji
Brush drawings by Mooji
Design by Rishi
Layout by Kiran

Printed in Canada

British Library Cataloguing in Publication Data.
A catalogue record for this book
is available from the British Library.

19   18   17

10   9   8   .7   6   5   4   3   2   1

How could I possibly describe my Master
when He is the source of all?
In Him all manifestation comes to life,
dances and goes back to silence,
yet He remains untouched.
He is beyond space
and is completely ungraspable
to the human mind.

He is the light of this world.
He gives life to life.

He creates the play of you and me,
of this and that, but He alone is.
He is subtler than space, lighter than light.
He is nothing with everything inside.
He alone Is.

From Him radiates tremendous peace,
silence and joy, but He is beyond all qualities.
All is Him alone.

Salutations to Thee.

Jai Sri Mooji!

– Krishnabai

"The Self is the only One.
If limited, it is the ego.
If unlimited, it is infinite.
It is the Reality."

Bhagavan Sri Ramana Maharshi
The Sage of Arunachala
Guru of Sri Poonja

"Don't touch anything that appears,
  because it will soon disappear.
  Look within to where
  there is no name or form
  and you will know who you are
  —Freedom."

Sri Harilal Poonja—'Papaji'

Beloved Papaji

Prostrations at the feet of my Master,
the embodiment of grace, wisdom and love;
the light of whose presence dispels all doubts
and delusion, thus establishing the mind
in its original state
        — Unborn awareness

Mooji

May all who come here in search of Truth,
and whose hearts and minds
beat only to discover the real,
come to the full realisation of the imperishable Self
inside their hearts and be timelessly happy and content.
Know that the true heart
and the illumined mind are one.
God and Truth are similarly one.
Know and acknowledge this with your entire being.
Go in peace.
And may all those who meet you along the way
be touched and inspired by your light,
your loving kindness and compassion,
your wisdom and silent presence
and so come to discover Truth
through this sacred encounter.
For blessed is the one
whose life is the evidence of Truth.
May the power of Truth prevail
in all its glory and perfection
in the hearts of those who love and honour
the Supreme Being.
That is my heart's blessing for you,
that you will always recognise the ever-present Grace
that is your heart's divine activity.
And may your presence be a true introduction to the
face, light and love of the living God.

Amen
Om

Foreword

It is with great joy that we welcome you to step into *White Fire*—a collection of unsparing, direct and timeless wisdom from advaita zen master, Mooji.

It is said that white fire is the most fierce of all. It burns everything, even the ashes themselves. To be in the presence of Mooji is to step into such a fire, for although he is the embodiment of love, openness and compassion, Mooji's uncompromising approach to Self-realisation leaves no space for egoic tendencies, spiritual fantasies and misconceptions that lead one astray. Mooji is an end-of-game master and *White Fire* an end-of-the-road book.

In compiling this book, we asked those who move closely with Mooji to send us the sayings which most touched, guided, inspired and shook them to the core—those pointings which ultimately threw them back into the Heart-Self. They are satsang excerpts so compelling that they ignited inside the Beingness as they were heard, and in response were scribbled onto bits of paper, backs of hands, tapped into phones and searched for in audio recordings, lest they disappeared or were forgotten.

We are also tremendously privileged to have received quotes directly from Mooji's own notebook, and recorded those that were spontaneously uttered as we read, refined and edited over eight hundred bullets of wisdom received from the *sangha*. Many quotes came from impromptu talks that arose in unexpected places—during a morning walk, on a bus ride to the beach, after a meal or while planting a tree.

Since 2012, a dedicated team has been making these gold nuggets of pure Truth available to the wider community. Mooji's Facebook page exploded in response, with the membership increasing twenty-fold to over 300,000 members. The world, it seems, is thirsty for pure Truth in bite-sized portions, ready to be swallowed and assimilated fully. *White Fire* arose in response to this readiness and openness to Mooji's teachings condensed into pill form.

While the sayings are full of wise, direct and encouraging guidance, they are not for the faint-hearted seeker who is only looking to reinforce a spiritual identity or projections. For those who come with openness and a Yes in their heart for Truth, every saying is a potent pointing in itself—rich and ready to be chewed and swallowed. The essence of Mooji's pointings is contained in each quote, no matter what page you turn to, and as such, *White Fire* can be read freely and without bookmarks.

Mooji often says that to find Truth you have to be like the cow that jumped over the moon. Even to understand such an utterance, one must leave the egoic mind-field and its literalness, and enter the heart's orbit. One must jump over oneself, over the moon-mind, as it were, to enter the heaven of Self-realisation.

May the white fire in this book ignite within your heart, leaving only the clear space of pure seeing and being.

The Editors

Postscript: While editing words which emerge from silence, a certain broadness is required in terms of the use of language and grammar. One may notice an inconsistency in the use of capitalisation and some of the usual conventions of writing. Do not allow this to distract you from what the words are pointing to.

ॐ

Burn me like
This ॐ
White fire
Grace of God
Until nothing
Remains
but You.

Mooji

I come to call you home

I come to call you home. Those who have a place for my words or my voice inside their heart, you already know or you will soon come to this place. You will discover its completeness, its joy and its fullness. I have come to call you away from suffering, from fear, from a life of sorrow, into your own divine Being. I have not come to give you any stories so as to excite your imagination or to sign you up for some long course or to call you into some membership. I have come to show you the unchanging and ever-present Truth and to remind you that you are already That, you are not separate, that the sense of separation from God, from Truth, is mere imagination believed into existence. This is how suffering is born. Know it is possible to wake up out of this long dream.

There is no one person on this planet who is apart from the Truth in their heart. The world is so diverse and extreme in its expressions; the greatest good and the greatest evil is here, and in this diverse forest of existence, you must find your way home. Many voices come to call us. I take it we are here together because of the power of God, the power of love and the power of Truth acting upon our hearts. I have not come to call you halfway home, but to call you fully home. I love to watch the beings awakening from the hypnosis of conditioning, from the fear of both death and life, by recognising their true nature.

Take courage. Being free is neither difficult nor distant. I know it has often been conceived, perceived and presented to be rare, remote and difficult, but all that is delusion—a great seeming. I don't know why awakening happens in one heart so completely and in another there is some delay or postponement. I am not deeply concerned about this. But I know that the voice that calls you is true, and where you are being called to is real and true. Heaven is inside your own heart. This is why I am here.

I don't delight in the imaginary. I need nothing from your past. This is not how I know you. I don't know you through your story. I know you through your heart—through your own divine Being. It is all that really corresponds with me, and it is my true connection with you—not a connection formed through ideology or philosophy, but a connection with the living power of God. It is this that I respond to, and it is only this that I know. I can only remind you; I can only point to that. The rest must somehow come from you in response to my pointing in order to complete this yoga of true understanding.

Sometimes, a feeling of tiredness, lethargy and resistance comes, and I want you to be aware of that. Do not fight with that, but rather keep your attention in the place that I have been pointing to—the silence of being.

It is not I who makes satsang successful at raising the beings from the sleep of ignorance of the Self to the bright joy of awakening; it is us together—you bringing forward your own truthfulness, your own deep yearning and your thirst for righteousness. It is this that causes everything to come alive, to sparkle with new possibilities. In my view, there is nothing higher in the human kingdom than discovering our divine nature. As everything else is perishable, find that which is imperishable, and fall completely in love with That.

Don't go to sleep until the night of ignorance disappears forever. Remember, the light, peace and presence of the Lord shines inside your heart eternally.

We are One.
There is only one of us.

2

The Truth is so simple and pure,
it doesn't need to be taught or learned.
It needs only to be pointed out and recognised.

3

The way is not really a way. It is a depth.
It is not a distance.
It is a deepening into the stillness,
deepening in the unmoving.
It is not a walking journey.
Journeys are for the body and the ego-mind.
But listening takes you deeper into
the bliss of the unknowable.

4

The universal one
is not the one who travels around the universe.
It is the one in whose emptiness a universe can be seen.

5

We are studying life and gathering knowledge,
but true knowledge is wisdom of the non-dual Self.
It does not come through study but through
synchronicity of the 'I' with the Supreme Being.

6

If there is a healing to be done, that healing
would be to wake up. This is the greatest healing.

7

If freedom is your heart's desire,
say Yes to Truth without hesitation or compromise.
Say to the Lord of the Heart,
'Replace 'me' with You.
Rid me of ego and merge my mind in You.
If there is identity, replace this identity with Truth.
Let there be only oneness here.
Dispel any arrogance, any ego
and let me melt in You,
beloved Lord of my Heart.'

This Yes is very, very powerful when it comes
from the heart itself. It comes from the heart
and goes straight to the heart and sets off
a time bomb in the earth-bound mind.

This Yes without compromise is the divine Grace
that comes to guide you back to your original
innocence, to your timeless and limitless being.

8

Your own being created me in your life
to remind you of who you truly are.
Don't depend on me—use me.
Make use of this and come home.

9

Who knows the sweetness of abandoning oneself
at the feet of the Supreme?

10

In this life, what ought to be the most important
is our search for the Truth. Truth can never be merely
concepts or conditioning or belief. Truth is spirit and
life. It is what we are. It is our essential nature and
being. It has been so from before the beginning of time,
for Truth is timeless.

The veils of ignorance, delusion and identification hold
all the beings hostage, causing them to be distracted
from the Self and to fixate upon the fleeting things of
this world. It is simply this which causes suffering.

Here in satsang, these veils are being pulled
apart so that true knowledge and the clear light
of awareness alone shines. This is love, and true
and lasting freedom. It is available to everyone,
because we are already this. All that is needed is
to come with an open mind and open heart,
with this urge inside: I must be free in this life.

11

This very day, life will reveal
a taste of the miracle of your real existence.
Without expectations or projections,
simply be open for this.

12

Upon discovering your infinite Self,
you break free from the binding ropes
of time and separation
and shine as the indivisible
and timeless Being.

13

The password into this game of existence is 'I am the
body'. All beings purchased this idea first and the
intuitive sense of 'I' became mere flesh, blood and
conditioning. This belief, 'I am the body, the doer of
actions and the thinker of thoughts,' is the most costly
concept in existence because it exchanges freedom for
bondage. The concept and feeling of being bound was
then introduced through the mind, and we bought it.
But you can come out of this. A quick and direct way
out of this game is through the path of self-inquiry.

Who or what arises here in this body as the
feeling 'I am'? Really try to identify what this 'I'
is so that you become very clear about this. The
sense 'I', which is natural to you, can it really be
an object? And if so, what is perceiving it? Can
this be also perceived? Ponder deeply over this.

This is the door that all sages went through into freedom.

14

Everything comes right
when you are sitting inside your own Heart-Self.
When you become empty of identity,
you meet all as the Buddha.

15

Those who feel bored in life
are ever seeking entertainment for their minds.
The lovers of God are ever content and serenely happy,
for they are fed through the heart
and not through the mind.

16

Behind the facade of the person there is the Truth.
I can only encourage you to come all the way.
Jump overboard into the arms of the eternal.
Jump now!

17

People underestimate the power of Self-awareness.
It is the purest and most potent force in the universe
and yet few human beings are aware of it
as their fundamental nature.

Grace has come in the form of satsang so that
you may recognise and experience your greatest
discovery: unending peace, joy, wisdom and love,
and more than this, your timeless existence
as unalterable awareness itself.

18

We believe so much in the evidence of our senses,
which we take to be real,
but of the evidence of consciousness
we appear to know nothing.
If you only take yourself to be
flesh and blood and conditioning,
then you have not as yet entered life.
If all you know of yourself is your person
—a restless and dissatisfied state—
then you better come home.
The sooner the better.

19

Rumi says, 'Whatever brought me here
must take me home.'
Now I ask you, What is home?
How much distance to home?
How many kilometres from home are you?
Inquiring like this, one finds the home that
is distanceless and inseparable
from one's own Self.

20

Who can count how many lives we have tasted?
Look at the stars. How old are they?
And a star is not even sentient. You are sentient.
How can you be less in age than a star?
You don't know at all.
What you do know is that right now
you exist and are here.
All take this for granted.
However, what should be known
is what you are here *as*.
And if what you are here *as* is clear, who knows this?
You want to learn about so many things,
but about *yourself*, you are not sure.

21

The sense, sound or vibration 'I am' is the first born
—the first name and vibration
emanating from the Supreme One.
Leaving aside all 'otherness' and merging the attention
in the I-am-ness presence inside the heart,
sentient beings attain lasting freedom
from the binding chains of delusion.

22

To know yourself is not a knowledge.
It is only a discovery.
It is not an achievement.
It is not a possession.
Nobody possesses Self-knowledge.
If anything, you can perhaps say it is an exchange
of the non-self for the Self,
but who will receive the Self? No one.
That is why I say it is not an exchange.
This may sound like a riddle to you,
a mystery or a paradox,
but only if you listen with just your mind.
You will understand all of this easily in the
presence, guidance and grace of a liberated being.
Seek such company.

23

The nature of a true one is simplicity and innocence.
There is an innocence that can never be lost;
it can only be hidden.
It cannot be destroyed nor can it be removed.
It can only be masked by the dream of conditioning.
All these things are quietly being undone now.
Whatever is not right is being put right
due to your openness to peer into yourself
and offer your life up in service to the real.

24

Something that once seemed like such a bad move
you later realise brought a wonderful change.
Now you are moving in the realm of the unknown;
life is spontaneous, unpredictable, miraculous.
Such are the paths of the Buddhas.

25

Your life should not be okay.
Your life should be sparkling.
Happy, contented, complete.
A Buddha's life is not okay.
Krishna's life is not okay.
Ramana is not okay.
They are K.O. You understand?
They knocked out the nonsense of ego.
An 'okay' life should not be accepted
by any intelligent being.
You have to discover, or unclothe,
your own Buddha Self,
your own Christ Consciousness,
your own Shiva Being.
If you wish to know how,
come to satsang.

26

Know this: When you say 'I',
the true meaning of 'I' is joy, it is happiness, it is life,
and it is also the witnessing of life.
Enjoy what comes,
but don't worry about anything at all.
Just be happy, happy, happy.
Know that whatever happens in life,
the final point is that everything is fine.
All is fine.

27

Even if you became an astronaut
and discovered other planets,
it would not be as great as discovering
your own Self right here on earth.

28

What is the ego-mind's fear of awakening?
It is: Who wants a relationship with Miss Nobody?
Who will employ Mr No-Mind?
What kind of future is there for one who is desireless?
But I am reminding you that all these are the ego's
taboos, imaginings and attempts to distract you
from your ever-perfect nature.
In truth, your awakened life will be magnificent,
harmonious, joyous and complete.

Follow your intuitive sense of the divine within.
Welcome its presence and vibration. Like this, your
insight opens to fully recognise the real as your
own Self. The awakened heart invites and allows
the Supreme to shine its light upon this world.

The ego is like God's egg that must hatch open to bring
that divine light into the world. To hatch means to
discover one's real nature. Through one's own satsang,
something inside is maturing enough to be merged in
God. And remember, God is not different from you.
It is not like you move out and God moves in.
He is you. God is your truest Self—the supreme Self.
Keep saying Yes inside your heart
and fall fully inside the Beloved.

You say you don't want anything but freedom,
but when you don't want anything, you *are* free.

My mind is struggling with thought activity.
How to stop this?

Actually, the truth is that mind is struggling *as* thought
activity. Mind and thought activity are one and the same
thing. Do not be fooled by this. Even the one struggling
is itself a thought construct. Observe. Clarify.
Confirm you are none of this.

32

Whatever comes, do not push away;
whatever goes, do not grieve.
Everything appears just like clouds floating by;
they just come and go.
Stay only as the unmoving awareness.
Awareness and Truth are one.

33

There is only one thing to be done:
Give up the idea that you are your personality
and be open to a greater Truth.
Spirit is presence, not person.
Like this, Grace enters your heart and reveals
your true nature as unborn awareness.

34

Wide are opinions,
narrow is experience
when perceived by the mind.
Narrow are opinions,
wide and deep is experience
when perceived by the Heart.

35

When man looks for experience he becomes the body.
When he looks for knowledge he becomes the mind.
When he looks for God he becomes the Heart.
When he looks for Truth he becomes Nothing.

36

When you are absolutely nothing,
you find galaxies of love,
worlds of peace, oceans of joy.
It is a paradox that you have to
give up everything to find everything.
That is what Christ means when he says,
'He who loses everything, finds everything.'
The one who gives up his life for Truth
finds everlasting life.
Now you have to solve
some of these ancient paradoxes.

37

Know and understand that you are not a 'person'
with consciousness, but rather,
the perceiver of such identity
and whatever else appears.
Whatever arises is seen
and intuitively discerned to be fleeting.
That which perceives cannot be that which is perceived.
Recognising all appearances to be impermanent by
nature, one ceases imparting reality to them.
Thus, one discovers and confirms
one's true place as the formless
and neutral witness
of all phenomena.

38

To be happy and unattached is the best.
To be happy and attached is rarely stable.
You may enjoy a relationship, a place, or some favourite
thing, but if you are attached, it means you are not
really free, you see. Now, to enjoy without attachment is
very rare indeed. Attachments often create expectations,
projections, dependencies, clinging and consequently,
suffering. Who has not tasted this? When the thing you
desperately desire is not available, suffering rains like
hot sulphur from the skies. The wise *really* know this.

39

Turn yourself entirely over to God or to the Master.
Otherwise you retain a self
who lives with a stolen teaching
and your ego creates a distorted version of the Truth,
and there begins your downfall.
But the one who surrenders everything in the first place
becomes empty and does not need to imitate anything.
Their whole life becomes the direct expression of God.

40

Your attitude should be:
If only one in a billion finds the Truth,
that one will be me.

41

For many years I worked as an artist,
but even while I was producing my best painting,
I myself was a living work of art
unfolding by the hands of God.

There is only the one Self.
An unchanging, unmoving silence.
It is not waiting, and it is not contemplating.
It is not reflecting.
It is not inquiring.
It is not resting.
All this could be perceived as modes of the mind itself.
What is that which is not in gear?
It is not a state. It is not in between states.
It is not the gap between thoughts. It is not a gap.
It cannot be done or undone.
For itself, there is no such thing as practice;
no such thing as contemplators,
meditators or attainers of it.
Hidden, yet nothing can hide it.
Revealed, yet nothing can see it.
Self-knowing, yet it is without knowledge.
Self-realised, yet it is without mind.
Blessing itself, yet it is beyond duality.
Being, yet it is beyond being.
Unfathomable, unconquerable, ungraspable.
Who or what is there?
Beyond sin and beyond righteousness.
It announces itself as the sense 'I am' inside the body,
but it is even beyond 'I' and beyond body.
Ungraspable, yet attention and the pure intellect
may recognise and acknowledge it.
Being revealed but it is not revealing.
Recognising its all-pervasiveness, joy fills the heart.
Intelligence dances. Peace rejoices.
The universes prostrate themselves,
yet their Lord they cannot see.

43

Grace sometimes touches life in such a way
that one's whole being is set on fire so powerfully
that one becomes filled with a confidence and urge
to throw one's whole existence into the abyss of the Self.
You may find yourself saying, 'Remove everything.
Save nothing. Remove every falsehood from my being.'
Then everything is thrown aside,
including one's self, the 'thrower'.
Unexpectedly, one finds a sense of great unburdening,
a completeness, peace and quiet joy within one's heart.
Now there remains an effortless silence and stillness.
And it is not that there remains an 'I' that received this.
There is nobody to receive.
Inside one's being, one quietly knows:
I am neither a receiver nor a giver. I am no one.
And yet, one finds oneself saying, 'Thank you, Beloved.'

44

Initially, people don't easily grasp what I am pointing
to because they are used to hearing and following with
their mind. But I am not speaking to their mind; I am
speaking directly to their heart. It takes them time to
rediscover the ability to listen with the heart. When
they hear me inside, everything becomes light and clear.

The mind is habituated to carrying out instructions in
order to reach somewhere or to discover something
phenomenally. However, real understanding occurs in
the heart, which is not trying to accomplish anything. It
only reveals the ever-present and timeless Truth we are.

45

Attempting to understand consciousness
with your mind
is like trying to illuminate the sun
with a candle.

46

What is clear seeing? Even when dust is in your eyes,
you can see. You can see that you cannot see clearly.
Imagine a room that is completely dark—no windows,
no light. You go in, close the door and say, 'I can't see!
I can't see!' But you can see. You cannot see objects in
the expected way, but you can see darkness. Always
you see. You perceive somehow. Similarly, we expect
to find something when searching for the Truth, but
the Truth is not an object. It is the subject in front
of whom is seen the illusory object-self searching for
the Self it already is. It is like the lie hides the Truth,
but only from the lie, for Truth cannot be hidden.

47

Don't play ping-pong with your mind.
Simply stay as the detached witnessing presence.
Observe that when left alone, mind calms down by itself.
But don't wait for this to happen.
Just stay as the unmixed presence.
Perceive without interest or identity.
Stay as the Self.

48

If there is a silence for a 'you',
there is going to be chaos for the same 'you'.
Silence belongs to no one.
It is synonymous with the Self.
Silence is to the Self what fragrance is to the flower.

49

Just keep quiet. What it means?
'Keep quiet' is the same as honouring yourself.
When the mind wants to run, you stay put.
You are not the mind—know this.
When the ego wants to go to the red-light district
and calls, 'Come, come and play a little,'
you instantly detect the lie
and the temptation dissolves.
Your peace remains undisturbed.
That is what it means to keep quiet.

50

If the world, as it is ordinarily perceived and
experienced inside the human mind and ego,
was indeed real, then one would be pressed
to declare, 'Oh my God, we are really in deep
shit.' Luckily for us, the shit is only inside
our heads and can easily be flushed out by
satsang. Find out what satsang is—urgently.

51

There are many religions.
Each one believes it is the only one
but in reality there is only One,
and that One has no religion.

52

The ego always wants Truth when it is ready.
It says, 'I am ready now. I am pure and available.'
But Truth does not come when the ego is ready.
Truth comes when the Heart is ready,
because Truth and Heart are one.
You have to turn away from the ego.
Jesus himself says,
'Deny yourself, take up your cross and follow me.'
It means: Deny your personal self, deny your arrogance,
deny ego and its seemingly cosy little identity.
Drop it. Turn away from it. Don't give any energy to it.
And 'take up your cross' means what?
Whatever it is that life brings, attend to that,
but don't be asking for the fruits of it.
Don't be claiming any doer-ship of anything.
Just move because life compels you to move.
And like this you find yourself in the presence of God.
You don't know how. You cannot boast.
You cannot say, 'I meditated for 16 hours non-stop
and I didn't even breathe.'
You cannot say or do anything.
All happened by the Grace of God.

53

The one who surrenders everything, including himself,
and the one who finds nothing, including himself,
discover the same Truth.

26

The 'little' self always wants to know
if it has reached the true Self yet.
It wants to be able to say,
'I have reached it, I have done it.'
But the true Self does not know any such thing
as a little self or its achievements.

You are being reintroduced to the unknown,
and something seems uncomfortable with this.
Well, everything is the unknown and unknowable.
And when you come to me,
I will always tell you to stay as your Heart.
Then you will begin to experience the miracle of existence.
As yet, your mind does not know this miracle.
You must trust. This is where the real adventure begins.

I don't want to become anybody's good story
or to be a good read.
I'm here to kick you out
of your false existence, basically.

A young woman is walking through the forest
of existence on the eve of her wedding day.
Her heart is full of the joy of anticipation
as she plans the final arrangements. Just
a few hours to go before she is in the
arms of her beloved. She is ablaze with
dreams of love, future and prosperity.

Suddenly a hungry lion steps out onto the forest road,
and they are face-to-face. They are so close she can
feel his rumbling breath. He is salivating, dripping.
She is standing on the razor-edge of existence.
Instantly, all her dreams, hopes and aspirations vanish.
Even her beloved, the light of her heart, disappears.
There is neither future nor past nor self here.

Welcome the lion on your path.

I am never talking about tomorrow, yesterday
or even today. I am pointing only to the timeless now.
Here there is not the concept or anticipation of 'next'.
Only the full awareness of being and presence.
No intention, no investment here. None needed.
If there appear any plans, they are only sketches
and all sketches are made in pencil.
Everything erasable, everything changeable,
and yet one's being is neither fickle nor flimsy.
Here.
There is a strength, but also a lightness.
There is power, but also softness.
There is firmness, but also flexibility.
The being is like solid emptiness.
Immeasurable.
Weightless.
Yet more solid than a mountain.
Lighter than space.
Full yet empty.
Sublime.

Just a very thin veil keeps that necessary sense
of individuality functioning now.
Beautiful.
It need not be lost.
One's being simply becomes like space moving in space.
My words are not a promise, just a pointing.
Sometimes I may say the Self is like a feelingless feeling.
Yet, in truth, it cannot be described at all.
The being is without story. Just the subtlest vibration.
That vibration itself is presence.
That vibration and joy are one and the same.
That vibration and peace, same-same.
That vibration and contentment are, similarly, the same.
But paradoxically, there is witnessing
to the vibration, to presence.
Who is there?

59

Leaving the person behind, in what time zone are you?
What date? What astrological sign applies to you?
Far, far beyond such things is your real being,
yet no distance is involved. Look.
You are not 'becoming' this,
you are not becoming anything at all,
yet the sense of becoming can arise.
Still, you are beyond that also.
Here, in your sizeless, weightless being, who are you?
For even the sense 'I am' is a phenomenon here.
Where are memories, and for whom,
in the vastness of being.

60

How can you come out of you?
There is no room.
Where will you land?
It's just an idea.

61

This so-called 'common' life in and around you will
be transformed into a miracle when the eyes cease
belonging to or working for the person and are
spiritualised through Grace and true understanding.
Even at this very moment this is already so,
for the timeless cannot be altered by the play of the
body-mind. There remains only that one wakes up
to one's inner reality as Truth itself.

Acclimatise yourself to Home.
Acclimatise mind to Heart.
Mind's true home is the Heart.
Not merely the emotional heart,
but the mind's source itself.
Heart is the guru of the mind.
Mind is the devotee of the Heart.
This is the true relationship.

You ask how to maintain this joy of being.
But I have to ask: How do you maintain being 'you'?
There is no one to maintain anything.
All happens spontaneously.
If someone had to maintain any state,
you would have to keep replacing them,
because they could not keep up
with the pressure of maintenance.

We don't like some human beings because they reflect something we don't like inside ourselves. We think it is in the other, but actually we carry this trait ourselves. Now, if you were empty of this trait that you don't like, you wouldn't judge it. When you are free of that judgement, the trait ceases to appear, even external to you. You don't see it, or at least you look towards it with great compassion and understanding, because you know it is not intentional. We are not really ignorant by choice. It seems like something is hiding the real seeing. So when you meet someone whose presence triggers discomfort within yourself, often it is because there is something there within you worth reflecting upon.

Now I take you a step further than this. This which you are seeing in others and in yourself, this self that you find fault with, is only the idea you have of who you are and its own conditioning. It is not the true Self. It is only the acquired state, the learnt or constructed self. This is where all the bad smell is coming from.

Rather than rejecting those encounters,
the wise welcome them.

65

Sometimes God challenges you
to find strength you don't have.
Only like this will you go beyond
your imagined limits.
You must be pushed so far
that you are forced to be humble.
Only then, when your pride and arrogance are
crushed, will you discover muscles that are not yours.
You will find and use the muscles of God.
When you completely abandon yourself, your ego,
this miracle becomes possible.

66

If you feel yourself in any form of 'I',
take it for granted that awareness is its root.
'I' sprouts from awareness, shape-shifts in awareness
and subsides in unchanging awareness.
This 'I' is the child of the Absolute.

67

Often due to the directness and power of satsang,
deep insecurities and attachments get exposed,
and many people experience the reflex to protect
a sense of vulnerability by running away.
This happens particularly at the start of intense
introspection. The paradox is that the thing
they are running away *with* is the very thing
they should be running away *from*.

Egoic identity is kept alive through habit, practice
and the unquestioned assumption that we are our
body and mind conditioning. We are living with
the notion that we are the constructed self. This
constructed identity is our root belief and nearly all
our activities spring from there. And we keep all
this up because it is all we believe we are. We are
faithful and loyal to this habit of associating with
impermanence, and like this we become a loyal member
of the community of ignorance. But once the ego is
immersed in the energy field of satsang, its power
and influence begin to thin away quickly. As soon as
the ego enters the Heart's orbit, it is like a meteorite
vanishing in the atmosphere before it reaches earth.

Identity cannot be neutral.
If it were to be neutral,
it becomes consciousness.

Always the perceiver will escape
every trick and trap of the mind.
In fact, for the formless perceiver,
there are no traps.

71

No need to believe or disbelieve. Don't interfere.
You can't improve the already perfect.
Just stay quiet and empty—let life play.

72

There is something powerful
in being rendered powerless.
It will break your arrogance
and possibly set you free.

73

We are standing here together and now you say you
wish to truly meet with me. So, it is clear that two
bodies, even in close contact, does not amount to
a meeting of the kind you wish. I am also open to
explore such a meeting, but I don't wish to meet you
as merely a psychological person. Apart from the
sense of a personal, psychological identity, is there
actually anything there to meet? Let's find out.

In fact, let us not overrate the idea of a meeting, because
to meet is not the ultimate. Meeting is already late.
Something is here before meeting. Can that which
exists before any concept be met? . . . And by whom?
Contemplate this.

74

You believe thoughts,
therefore you become easily confused
and so peace is hidden.
Behind the screen of mind
is the realm of unchanging awareness
—silent, vast and perfect.
The wise leave aside
the incessant murmurings of the mind
and merge themselves here
in the infinite stillness of Being.

75

If there is an 'I' who can 'get it',
there will be an 'I' who can 'lose it',
and this 'I' is nothing but thought.
When believed in, it is the most costly thought,
for it exchanges inhibition for your spontaneity
and complexity for your innocence.

76

Emptiness is effectively the absence of you.
And where there is the absence of 'you',
there shines the presence of God.

77

I am nobody.
I know nothing and am nothing.
      Such complete joy.

78

The ego-mind looks for what it can get.
Heart-mind looks for how much it can give.

79

You have to see and meet God in this life.
Don't let this life go by
and miss discovering the Supreme One.
You will find him inside as your constant being.
Pray: Holy mother, holy father, holy spirit,
don't give me the illusion
that even one second belongs to me.
All is you. I also am you and yours.
Only like this is one's life transformed
into the miraculous.

80

When will you admit that you are the Infinite?
By the way, where are you?

81

Everything is in you, including me.
And everything is in me, including you.
And yet neither you nor I exist.
Who will catch this clue?

82

Emptiness is the root. Always come back to this. It is
the key, the door and the space of freedom. From here,
everything becomes easy to understand, to assimilate.
Here, presence, understanding and action are one.
Your understanding reveals your oneness with the
great harmony, which is taking care of everything
already. You just get the front row seat to observe all
this. If you are the person, you will have to do the
donkey work. You have to think, listen, act and wait
for the result, then hee-haw! Celebrate . . . or not.

When you perceive from and as the Heart, you
realise that the show has been happening perfectly
all along. Just you were looking at it with imperfect
eyes and identity. It is not that suddenly the world
starts to work more in your favour, like you become
God's VIP. No. It is already there and it has always
been there—perfect. But you didn't see it, because
you were living with an ill-conceived idea of reality.

83

I am not looking for right answers.
I am looking only for You.

84

The ego-mind is not strong, it is you as a person who is weak. Actually, as the Self, you have all the power. If the mind is strong, it is only because it has sucked all your strength due to the scholarship you grant it. Remember, it has no power of its own. It runs only on phantom power—you supply the juice. Without your interest, the mind is like a cut flower, soon to wither away. Grieve not.

85

Don't be a storehouse of memories.
Leave past, future and even present thoughts behind.
Be a witness to life unfolding by itself.
Be free of all attachments, fears and concerns
by keeping your mind inside your own heart.
Rest in being.
Like this, your life is always fresh and imbued
with pure joy and timeless presence.
Be happy, wise and free.

Even if at times you feel you have done the worst thing
imaginable or that the whole world is against you
or rejects you, even if you feel no one understands
you, loves you or accepts you, do not entirely trust
your mind. Do not think it is on your side.

Know this: you never have to apologise for your
existence. You are not here by accident but by the
will and love of the Supreme Lord of the universe.

You are not merely 'living' life; you are life itself
and also the witness of life. All challenges in life
arise to motivate, mature and direct your mind
towards true wisdom. Thus, by opening your heart
to Truth, they stimulate and inspire you to go
beyond the inhibited personal self and its projections,
misconceptions and false beliefs. Ultimately
challenges lead you, through Grace, to discover
your real nature and Self as unborn awareness.

What I truly am is not merely a state
that is visited during meditation.
Usually, meditation is aimed at reaching me, the Self
who observes the act of meditation and its intention.
I am unreachable.
I am pure and unchanging awareness,
the absolute reality. I alone Am.
All that is perceivable is my fragrance only,
but I, the untouched flower, nobody can pluck.

88

In satsang we are exposing and discarding the unreal.
When the unreal is discarded,
you don't have to go and search for the real.
The real alone remains. It is ever here.
You realise it never left.
It is always here as your own Self.

89

Yours could be a tongueless spirituality so that your
very presence exudes the perfume of God. We are
too good with words. When we study so much, we
separate the Self and make it into a distant goal.
Then we write big fat books on consciousness, super
consciousness, super-duper consciousness. So of
course people say, 'Oh my God. I cannot even get
to the first stage of consciousness. How will I move
beyond?' Simplicity is not so attractive to the human
mind, which wants shining stones and crystal caves.
You imagine a didgeridoo vibrating on your stomach
will heal all your bullshit. So we fancy all this stuff,
but the Truth we don't give a second glance—it's far
too simple and effortless for your complex mind.
Could we meet in such simplicity?
In fact, there lies your magnificence.

90

Sayings are only strong if you swallow them.
The medicine only works if you take it.
The timeless destroys time and the one who lives it.

91

Once you begin to recognise the divine gifts in life,
you come to see that there are so many.
Your life is abundant.
Every moment is an opportunity
to rest in effortless Self-awareness.

92

To leave yourself aside is the greatest thing,
but it will seem impossible in the beginning
because as an ego you have always been
your own favourite person.
Your favourite person in the world is yourself
and you love to serve yourself best.
But now a joy is arising each time we deny ourself
in favour of serving others.
This gap between 'you' and 'me'
begins to diminish somehow.
First, it was 'me' and 'the rest',
then 'me' becomes 'we'.
Ultimately, a realisation dawns: we are one.
The sage within us emerges when the 'we',
the 'me', and finally, the 'you' and 'I' disappear.
There remains only the all-ness,
the one beyond even the concept of oneness.

93

When you awaken to your harmony with God,
you will see that all things are already
flowing within the same harmony. No need for a separate doer.

94

Just learn what you can and leave the rest. Do not
dwell on old mistakes or missed opportunities, for this
sustains personal identity and drains the being of its
freshness. Remember, none can live a fault-free life.
Accept this. It is okay. It is the programmed mind that
gets caught up in the sludge of morality. Don't empower
those tendencies further. It is not necessary nor is it
required to make any oath, vow or pledge in your life,
because few can fulfil them and they just become a
burden around your neck. Recognising your true place
as the uninvolved witness is your door to freedom.

95

If you only want a bit of Truth, it will take a lot of effort.
If you desire the complete Truth, it will be effortless.
If you wish to go part of the way, it may take you forever.
If you choose to go all the way, it will take no time.
If you are burning for Truth, it may just be you
who will recognise the Infinite.

96

You say, 'I am a doctor. I am a yogi.
I am a vegetarian. I am forty.'
You assume you know the 'I' that claims all these things.
But do you truly know the 'I' that am?
The true 'I' is none of these things.
Recognise the unassociated 'I am'
—this alone is complete and true.

97

Let everything in the mind play in this world of duality.
God is playing as everything, everything, everything.
Don't think some things are more God and others are
less. Have the attitude that everything is God, including
yourself. With this attitude, you're really beginning
to recognise and feel God inside your being.

If you think God is never going to forgive you
for things, this is somebody else's idea.
This is not of God. Truth is nothing like that.
These are the things you have to forget about.

98

There will come a point when you find
an ocean of peace inside you that will never leave you.
Noise will come, but it will come inside your peace.
Noise will go, but peace will not go.
Once you discover this peace,
you won't buy any of the mind's promises.

99

Many have long believed in the second coming of Christ,
but why only second? Why not the third, the fourth,
the thousandth, the ten thousandth coming?
For each one who trusts in his words
and is absorbed in his spirit
becomes a door through which he comes.

With this body, you have the experience
of time, taste, smell, touch
—the taste of otherness, of beauty.
But I want you to come deeper in,
beyond the field of the transient.
Your attention was going out through the senses.
Now we press the reverse button.
Make a U-turn and come inside as far as you can
but carry nothing with you.
Now go beyond the facade of the body,
beyond emotions, feelings, thoughts.
Dive deeper and deeper inside, bypassing all phenomena
—family, education, culture, conditioning, self-image.
Very good. Now come even more inside . . .

Silence.
Still come past silence, come more in.
Confirm the place beyond which you cannot go.
Be here.
And now what happens?

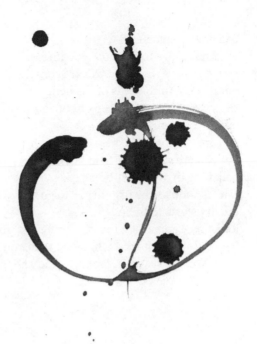

Look with the fullness of yourself,
not just with your eyes.
'Here there is nothing!' you say.
And I ask, Is there anything beyond nothing?
What perceives nothing itself?
Look deeply.
The human being must go through
one door after another,
and each and every door closes behind him
until he comes here.
Now you are here, inside the inside itself.
You are this nothingness
experiencing itself beyond duality.
Rare is a human being
who abandons himself in order to come here
—the place of the unborn.

101

You have to get cured.
The knowledge has to cure you inside.
You may have the sense you are consciousness,
but it is not in the cells of the being as yet.
We have to wash the sleep out of your eyes,
out of your being.
You are the consciousness already,
but you are still in the field of duality
believing in non-duality.
And as soon as the urge arises to go beyond duality,
duality starts to fight.
Resistance comes, trying to capture lost ground.
It's a bit of a fight for a while, but then you are reminded:
What you are searching for is already here.

102

To win is to be One.

103

Sometimes you feel you are knowing less and less,
but actually something is expanding more and more.
You are experiencing more of yourself
although you didn't become anything at all.
These are paradoxes that cannot be easily explained.
Trust.
You are coming to the edge of your personal existence,
and are falling into the abyss of your own Self.
Say inside your heart: I am here for this alone.
In choosing freedom now, it is chosen forever.

Mooji gives blessings during his visit to Mooji Satsang Bhavan, Rishikesh, India 2016

Mooji prostrates at the bed of his Master, Papaji, in Lucknow, Uttar Pradesh, India 2016

Coming from the holy Ganga River at Vasishta's cave, Uttarakhand, India 2014

The True Life

Without the intrusiveness of personal mind, life is observed to be unfolding in a natural and harmonious way. Do not waste time just wishing for things to get better. The whole world is doing this and no one is really happy. We miss the true life. In fact, happiness arises when you stop chasing for something other than your own pure nature, and this is the happiness that remains with you.

The universal tendency in human beings is to seek lasting happiness in the field of names and forms, a transient field. Because they believe this is all there is, they look for happiness by immersing themselves in experience after experience, therapy after therapy, workshop after workshop—even 'spiritual' ones, which all sound so promising but never really address the present. This is really a form of avoidance, a distraction from what is timelessly unchanging and ever-perfect within ourselves. Ignorance of the Truth is the main cause of misery.

Avoid expectations and especially be aware of the tendency to wait for 'next' as a promise to happiness—the next good feeling, the next adventure or invitation from the mind. The 'next' experience, in fact, does quite the opposite; it pulls your attention away from pure presence, the seat of joy.

No one has ever experienced 'the future'. Reflect. It is all imagination. How to transform these tendencies? Simply begin by paying attention to the natural thought-free state, the pure sense of existence, the feeling 'I am' that is naturally present in you. Shift the attention away from the mind-traffic and let it rest in impersonal awareness. Keep doing this each time the attention goes out towards sense objects or obsessive self-interest.

Self-attention is the beginning of real Self-discovery. It returns the attention time and again to its source—the one Self. Get used to staying in your natural and neutral state of being, a state of emptiness. Do not be afraid of this. In fact, get increasingly used to being empty. This emptiness and joy are synonymous. They are one. This is really what is meant by the saying, 'To enjoy one's self.' It is a state of unfading contentment, wisdom, love and happiness.

Mooji, you speak about not looking for the next experience, but I feel so much better after reading self-help books and participating in courses. I really do feel that I am growing and evolving spiritually towards the Truth you point to.

Trouble will come from your belief in this 'self' that you aim to improve. This is strong for people because one of our most treasured beliefs in this life is in personhood. Satsang is the biggest threat for the 'person'. In authentic spirituality, satsang is a sword. It is such a direct way to expose the unreality of this little person-self. My words may at times seem brutal or even unkind, because you actually think you are doing so well, but from my place of looking, you are actually drowning in delusion while dreaming you are close to freedom. All this is the mind's deception. You cannot be free as a person. You can only be free *from* the person. If the sickness is strong, the medicine must be equally strong; we are not talking about simply changing clothes, but about forces that can oppress your mind and send it into hell.

When I speak like this, people may react and take offence, but it is actually a chance of resurrection into eternal life.

If your heart stops, sweet words are not going to get it beating again. You need a powerful shock. Sometimes it is not enjoyed, and I know how it is felt, but some delusions have to be crushed immediately, directly and without compassion—which incidentally is true compassion. If you do it slowly, you end up protecting the very thing that is suffocating your being. If you merely prune at your troubles, you will end up tit-for-tatting with me. I am not here to give opinions or exchange concepts. I speak with the authority of my own experience, which is not personal, and because it is not personal it has authority. The one who is personal has no authority for me; they cannot challenge what I am speaking. They can resist it, but they cannot challenge it authentically because the ground that they stand on is quicksand. When we are identified with the ego, we have no power—we have deluded power, aggression perhaps, but never the power of God.

People need to wake up and climb out of the strangling hole of egoic identity, to re-embrace the power of the living God within themselves. Rise up into a life of joy and peace; leave behind sorrow, vain investments and delusions. So I don't come lightly. I come with love, but I don't always come with a bouquet of flowers. I come with a sword, a loving and living sword. People don't see or appreciate a loving sword—until their head falls off. Such is the power of Truth.

104
Don't make the mistake of imagining
that the Divine judges the world by human standards.

What chance is there to discover the final Truth?

Here with me, every chance, because I don't accept
you in the way you present yourself. This self-portrait
I disregard. It is a poor work of art or heart.
You want to be here as Mr and Mrs Sannyasin,
Mr and Mrs Hormone, Mr and Mrs Spiritual,
Mr and Mrs Special, Mr and Mrs Chosen,
Mr and Mrs Yogi . . .
I'm sorry, not here. I have no space for you.
Try again another time, or maybe another life.
When you run out of titles, come back.
But who will take up this offer?

Before a thought arises, do you know it is going to
come? You cannot decide, 'Oh, I'm only going to
have Jesus-thoughts today,' or, 'I dedicate this space
for only Buddha's words and thoughts this week.'

Thoughts arise arbitrarily and unannounced, but this by
itself is not thinking. Thinking begins when the arising
thought connects with the thinker-thought, the thinker-
identity. Out of this communion, thinking is produced.
Know that both the thinker of thought and thoughts
are one: mind. When it is seen that the thinker-thought
construct is a concept, the play of the psychological mind
ceases to engage your attention and peace prevails.

107

O Lord, wash away every seed
of poisonous duality and identity
so that inside here is only You.

108

You are both the 'what is' and the 'what will be',
but the 'what will be' is imagined, ephemeral,
arising like clouds in the sky.
The clouds are many but the sky is one.
Don't try to be cloud or sky.
Be that nameless space
sometimes referred to as Nothing.

109

You say you are truly tired of searching and techniques.
All you want now is to find and be the awareness,
but I want to ask you, Who exactly are you, the one
who is trying to find awareness? Is not this effort
and the one trying to do it perceived as a transient
appearance inside the very awareness oneself truly
is? I see the delusion of this one and you are going
to see it too if I have anything to do with it. It is
only a question of whether you are up for it or not.
Why do I have this confidence? Because I know,
beyond doubt, that you are the Buddha Being.
My eyes can only see That.

110

Paying attention to the momentary appearance
of the mind is called distraction.
Distraction means to turn away
from our ever-present Self.

111

We strain to attain the effortless. We get up, shower,
dress in nice clothes only to throw out the trash.
In the same way, we overwork the mind in pursuit
of the effortless, missing all along the fact that we
are already the thing we are seeking. Why all this
craziness? The mind is very happy to create an
imagined journey, a journey we believe in. But how
can it get close to the Self? The Self has no distance.

112

Do you really want to erase all your deluded beliefs,
memories, stories, tendencies and identities one by one,
or would you prefer to find the factory where they
are produced and blow the whole thing up?
I say this because right now
I don't have time for all this tiny pruning.
You hold onto your little nail clipper,
but I am giving you a great chainsaw
to bring down the whole tree of suffering.
This chainsaw is self-inquiry.

113

Carry nothing and be carried by tireless Grace.

Beloved
Remember
Love without clinging
Give without demanding
Receive without possessing
Perceive without projecting
Witness without judging
Focus without tension
Work without strain
Relax without laziness
Play without competing
Enjoy without craving
Reflect without imagining
Serve without demonstrating
Surrender without hesitating
Challenge without dominating
Meditate without identity
Correct without blaming
Overcome without pride
Master without enslaving
Laugh without cynicism
Cry without pity
Confront without hatred
Guide without superiority
Enter without self-importance
Depart without regret
Live without arrogance
Exist without self-image
Be one with God
Awaken to the Real

115

Many spiritual practices are pleasant.
They don't challenge your identity and its delusion,
therefore they are attractive to your mind.
There's nothing threatening when someone tells you,
'We're chanting because it purifies the energy
and brings you closer to God.'
It feels nice for people—adventurous and agreeable.
But I'm not interested in adventure,
I'm here only for liberation!
Not entertainment for your mind,
but the smelling salts that will
stun you into awakening.

116

Reject everything for a moment and come to that
which cannot be rejected, for that alone is complete.
When you are one with this recognition, all becomes
pure and clear. Only then are you able to exhale the
collected tensions and burden of conceptualisation.

117

All human encounters appear from outside
and are consolidated within.
But the Lord unveils himself from inside our hearts
as the supreme source of our existence
and shines there forever.

118

You have never been a person,
and yet you have been so many people.
So many versions of the single Self you have tried,
and yet all your efforts have failed to make real
what is merely imagined.
Don't stop at the person.
There is a space behind the person,
beyond the person.
This space is you.

119

If you wish to find love,
don't look for the object of love,
look instead for the source of love,
for there you will meet and merge
with the Beloved—your inmost Being.

120

You are here perceiving.
You cannot be the things perceived,
as they all come and go.
If you were an object of perception,
when the object goes, you would also be gone.
But you are still here to watch this
and every other thing go.
Who are you?

Papaji said, 'To discover Truth,
you will have to disappear.'
Now, who was he speaking to?
How do you disappear?
Can 'you' do it?
Who could carry out such an instruction?
Actually, nobody can.
It was not even an instruction
but the words detonated like a grenade inside my being.
Sometimes the Master says things 'you' cannot do.
It is one of his most powerful teachings,
a teaching no one can follow.
Grace alone does it.

Expansion and contraction are only movements in you.
You are unaffected by the movements of time or change,
yet fully alive within your own Self,
needing no descriptions nor assistance.
The Self is unchanging, ever present,
without desire, without fear.
Here you need neither courage nor faith
nor hope nor trust.
Whether it is night or day
does not concern you here.
You are not creating nor imagining,
but simply discovering and melting
into the silence of Being.

Grace is everything.
Grace is another name for what we are.
Grace is indefinable, the ever perfect, timeless.
It is that in which the apparent timeful plays
as names and forms in their brief dance as life.

We are the experience and simultaneously
the witness of this experience.
Grace is that which calls you away from the chaos,
away from the noise of the world.

Grace is the same as peace,
but there is no peacekeeper
nor anyone being silent.
Grace is the breath of the Self.

124

Be where seeing arises from,
where even the seeing is being seen.
Just be there. This is your home.

125

Life does not worry about life.
Only mind does that.

126

If something seems to be blocking the recognition
of our true Self, I wonder if it is simply the
loyalty, the addiction, that we as consciousness
have developed towards our projected identity
as a person. Just this identity—which in fact
doesn't even exist—when believed in, is enough
to give the sensation of blocking the Infinite.

Now, this is the most powerful delusion on earth:
something that does not exist covers and hides
the Supreme Lord of the universe.
But hides him from whom?
Who, if not himself, wears the mask
of 'other', 'me' or 'I'?

127

How fortunate are the lovers of God
who are privileged to abandon themselves at his feet.
Even for the one who lives under God's toenail,
such shelter, such abundance!

As soon as you recognise your true nature as the
unchanging awareness and confirm your position
as that itself, it won't matter anymore what the
psychological, personal mind is saying. Its play
and presence will become distant—like looking at
the moon in full daylight. You won't be listening
to it for very long, I tell you. It will gradually
lose its influence and appeal and drop away.

Now, as the old tendencies flare up again,
do not lose heart. Do not say, 'When will I ever be free?'
Take courage. Take the attitude, 'This is my chance.
Thank you for yet another chance
to make my stand inside you, O Beloved.'

130

What can the moon give to the sun?
Can the moon say, 'Sun, you are not bright enough.
Let me give you a little bit of my light'?
What can the mind give to the Heart?
What can the mind give to the Self?
Mind's job is to prostrate to the Self.
Mind should be the devotee of the Self, nothing else.
You are the Self. Stay as the Self.

131

A lot of things I don't know about,
but I know in the moment I need to know.
And the things I don't need to know,
I am not concerned about.
This is my good fortune.

132

To be nothing is the greatest freedom.
In fact, when you are nothing,
there is not even freedom,
for where is the one who is to be free?
Reflect upon this.

133

Transcending the 'I' concept,
all is perceived in and as the Self alone.

Don't belong to anything.
Don't belong to anyone.
Just be.

Feel your being first and foremost,
and don't compare or compete.
Just be your being.

Focusing on your person
creates a distraction from the Truth.
Focusing on the presence
does not take you out of yourself
but guides you back to the source—absolute awareness.
For now, don't focus on you, focus on me.
When you focus on you,
it is only a focus on your person or ego.
Focusing on me returns you to your own source
where we are one.

In front of some intelligence,
this game of existence is being acted out.
But there is a seeing place
that is beyond every category.
It doesn't belong to any religion, political party,
spiritual discipline, race or gender; nothing at all.
Everything happens in front of it,
and this you have to find.
This recognition will shatter all your doubts
as you are being replaced with
the inseparable Self.

137

True silence cannot be kept. It can only be discovered.

138

Sometimes, knowing 'how' is the worst thing
because it goes straight to the mind's bank account.
Mind seems to want to know how to find the Self
so it can remember how to go there next time.
Actually, it is leading you deeper and deeper into
the forest of delusion, for it is an unreliable guide.

You want to discover the Truth. You don't need to
know how. Knowing how means I have to teach you
some technique, but instead I will go with you. I will
walk with you right now. You don't need to know
how. You don't need to know anything at all actually.
Just accept my words.

139

No one, no situation or circumstance, nothing at all
can, by itself, prevent you from being your true Self.
Drop this foolish and costly belief and rest fully in
the house of inexhaustible freedom, wisdom and love
—your Father's kingdom.

140

In the absence of you personally
is the presence of you universally.

All beings are bitten by the serpent of ignorance.
But when ignorance combines with arrogance,
then we are really in a very bad state.
You have to come out of arrogance.
When arrogance goes, humility comes.
When humility comes, ignorance also will go.
When ignorance and arrogance are no more,
Grace will be recognised and experienced
as the pure presence of God.

In satsang, something gets emptied out.
All the old ideas are thinning away.
The mind itself goes into *samadhi*, it becomes empty.
And there is a beautiful silence in your being now.
Get used to it.
The mind is cunning. He may say, 'I did it!'
Don't accept this voice. No one did anything.
Don't identify with thoughts, words or feelings.
Simply keep quiet. This is the final cut
to the umbilical cord of the ego-mind.
Cut him loose without compassion.
Let him go and the great silence is here,
seamless and untouched.
Sit inside your undivided Self.

143

'Find me,' says the holy one,
'find your retreat in me.
Find me within.
You are never apart from me.
You have been with me
since before the creation of the worlds;
every form you have appeared in,
I have been there with you,
in the centre of your being.
Until now you've missed me,
yet I, the source, am always here.
We are one.'

144

Happiness is your nature,
effortlessness is your dance,
peace is your fragrance,
love is your perfume.

145

What would you want to hold onto
when you have no future?
Which, incidentally, you don't.
And you without past, future or even present,
you are the Real.

You say you want to find the Truth.
But it cannot be done.
What actually happens is that
as you are looking for your factual self,
the identity you are looking with begins to disappear.
Like a falling star that disappears
before it touches the earth,
nothing remains but the immutable and
formless awareness space—the Self.

The power of the Supreme is so great,
it allows you to be nothing.
There is no need to be somebody.
No need to prove anything.
And this is the greatest love.

Don't save anything, including you.
This is the purpose of these conversations:
to flick out, to flush out, to scrape out
the last little bits of nonsense from inside.
Sometimes you think there is only a little thing to
remove, but it's all of you that needs to be scraped out!
This is the kind of emptiness I am talking about.
Here, you have already touched base;
you have no opinion,
no need for privacy or specialness.
The beautiful thing is that
the more you remove, the more you are.
This is the major scam you have to get out of.
The more you think you are losing,
the more in fact you are discovering
of your real Self, which is limitless.
You are exchanging this small ego-identity
for the immeasurable.
Otherwise, it's like you are hiding God . . .
but from whom?
God cannot be hidden.
All this is God's dream.

149

Be grateful for the mind whose role it is to molest
the false version of yourself until it becomes unbearable
and you are left with no choice but to give it up
and come Home.

150

My love, why all this worry?
There is only the infinite Self.

151

*You say to stay as awareness itself. Does this mean to
completely leave everything, even the desire to destroy the
vasanas, the deep-rooted tendencies of the personal self?*

Yes. Rather than focusing upon self-improvement or
fighting against the force of *vasanas*, which can seem
unending, one should directly find out to whom these
tendencies belong and who is affected by them.
Recognising that they belong to and attack one's
false self-image alone, and that one's real nature
is the unchanging awareness, the false identity
crumbles. Thus, one becomes immediately free
from delusion and attains clear-minded liberation.

152

It does not matter what comes up.
What matters is who you are, the one perceiving it.

Who gave us this crazy idea
that we should know how to live?
Does a tree know how to grow?
Does a cloud know how to float?
Does the wind know where it is blowing?
Does a road know it is going somewhere?
Don't know how to live,
just recognise that you are life and life just is.

154

When you come with an open mind, you notice
and enter easily the flowing streams of Grace. If
you cling to your projections, you will be oblivious
to this. In the same way that you cannot think two
thoughts at the same time, you cannot see the real
if you are intent on fulfilling your projections. From
the beginning of time, we have been perceiving
what we are conceiving and not what truly is.

155

Bodies are time bodies.
Not even the sages could keep them.
Give to time what belongs to time,
but you stay as no time.
The ways of the mind are ancient,
but your Self is timeless.

156

The sage sees only the Self.
The person sees lots of persons.
One sees from wholeness,
one sees from fragmentation.
Both are you.

157

The one who has merged in the unknown
does not need to know anything.

When not being your Self becomes far too painful,
Self-discovery becomes vital. It seems we can live in
exile from our own true nature for a while. It is the
play of life after all. Actually, we cannot do it. We can
only dream it, or believe it into existence and suffer
our own projection. Such exile would be akin to saying
that space has forgotten itself and imagines that it is
only the wind. Space imagining itself to be blowing
when actually it is only the wind that is blowing—what
delusion. When the wind is not blowing, does space
'become' space again? Is space not always unchanging?
Wind or no wind, what concern is that to space?
Likewise, you are only a person when you imagine
you are a person. When you cease believing you are
a person, there is no person and no confusion. When
the wind is not blowing, who speaks of the wind?

You are none of this, O Divine Awareness.

159

The Lord of the universe dwells
inside the heart of every being
as unmixed presence.
This must be discovered not as mere teaching
but as direct and intuitive experience.

160

Perhaps God's greatest gift is to steal your mind
and leave you as pure awareness.

For you, the worst thing is to forget yourself,

whereas for me it is the best thing possible.

I'm a creative being, but I also want to be liberated in this life. How can I find a balance between these two urges?

Sometimes you delight in nice experiences and creativity, but like this you don't wake up to what you are. Don't let the art rule the heart. Don't invest your energies so fully into developing anything phenomenal, because what you are searching for is beyond even spirituality—it is the ever-present reality. Though it is ageless and imperishable, it is not an object and therefore cannot be kept, for even the keeper is ephemeral. All seeking is for objects, but the true seeking takes you back to your Self, the invisible and indivisible Being.

You may pour a lot of energy into your creative expression and regard yourself an artist. People may respond to your creative ability and even call you great. Your ego may grow, but you yourself stop growing, because too much energy goes to perfecting your art rather than being the heart itself. Creativity is to be enjoyed as a spontaneous expression of the consciousness, but creativity by itself does not lead to the discovery of one's timeless Being. The search for Truth is the ultimate impulse of sentient existence. However, Truth cannot be the reward at the end of any creative process, for Truth, as awareness itself, is that in which the very striving to create or to attain perfection in any field is perceived.

Giving up the attachment to everything,
including one's own self-image,
only the eternal, the imperishable remains.
This—we are.
In fact, this is the only true way to be with me:
discover and be one with the Truth
of your own impersonal Self.

Of all the things that human beings can learn in this life,
I have the greatest news to tell,
the most beautiful thing to share:
Find and rest in that which can never come to an end.

Best is just be nothing.
See if the mind can speak to you when you are nothing.
Invite this.

Live by the light of your own heart . . .
but make sure this heart is silent and empty.

167

There is nothing you need to do
to become what you are,
but there is something you need to recognise
in order to stop being what you are not.
Your complete nature is already here.
Remember that all that you perceive,
including your sense of self and personal identity,
is as ephemeral as clouds floating in the
unchanging sky. You can never not exist,
but through perfect understanding,
you will cease existing as what you are not.

168

When you can write your autobiography
on the back of a stamp and still have room to spare,
I wish to meet you.

169

The knowledge of the Truth is not a knowledge to keep.
Contrary to the mind's understanding of knowledge,
which is something to keep, to save and cherish,
true knowledge removes 'you'
and leaves an empty space.
And when there is no 'you', there is only Truth.
There is only the Supreme
appearing in the form of a human being.
Even now, we are the Supreme,
but the game is to know this consciously
without arrogance, pride and identity.
And this knowing is being.
They are one.

170

Beloved,
Let me never imagine I am something.
Let me never forget I am nothing.
What Grace you have showered upon my being
to have filled this space with You alone.

In order to really grow inside,
you must first be challenged from all directions.
Things cannot just go your way.
You cannot command life or expect
it to fulfil your projections.
If things are always easy,
you go to sleep inside your being.
As you become more sensitive,
more alert, intuitive, open and silent,
fear, resistance and lethargy subside
and are replaced with a deep calm
and a faith in the unseen one.
Though no outer company may be seen alongside you,
the one who walks with God is never alone.
The hosts of the heavens walk with them.
Welcome on the road of the true life.

Mooji, what is the difference between your 'I' and mine?

Nothing. Except the 'I'-sense in you seems to go out
and come in to the sense of a person, whereas here
it goes out from and comes back to nothing.

Don't pay attention to that which is coming and going.
If it seems important, then take a look. Don't be afraid.
If it can be ignored, ignore it.
If it cannot be ignored, bring it into the light of inquiry,
and confirm yourself as its formless witness.

Something is hiding, but I am here to tell you it
is not really you. It is your self-portrait, the idea
you have of who you are which you will carry until
you discover your true Self. The Self is without
shame, without blame. It is eternally pure.

Every human being has this eternal purity inside,
and in satsang, it is being unveiled. We are opening
the curtains of the body-mind identity to see
behind. Initially something is afraid of being seen
because we have an idea that underneath the surface
of our expression may be something bad. But the
awakened one sees this as another layer of illusion.

Is it that the person is real, but when you try and
be the awareness, somehow the person gets hidden
but is nevertheless still real? No. It was never real.
The person was made to seem real by our interest,
belief and identity. We feel like we are dealing
with real things, but nothing phenomenal has
inherent reality. What is really here is the Self.

A sheep had a dream of meeting a lion.
One day the dream came true.
You know what the result is.
There was only one left after such a meeting.
Who do you imagine it was?
The same thing is happening in satsang.
When the one who is seeking
finds what he is searching for,
he will be swallowed into That.
However, in this absorption,
he will be in the full awareness
that he is the untouched Self.
This is my clue.

Fire burns everything leaving only ashes.
But there is another fire so fierce
it burns even the ashes—White Fire.
Have this attitude:
'Burn me like this, O White Fire.
O White Fire, Grace of God,
consume me until nothing is left but You.'
I want to meet such a human being who can say this.
I long to be in such holy company.

177

We are too much in love with forms.
Don't just fall in love with forms,
not even with my form because one day it will also go.
Of course, by all means enjoy the forms,
for the Lord dwells inside them also.
Sri Ramana Maharshi and Papaji
are also alive in my heart
although their physical bodies are not present anymore.
But the Truth that they are is eternally alive in me
as it should be in you.

178

Taking care of the *sangha* is taking care of me.
Taking care of me is taking care of the *sangha*.

179

When you discover the *here* which is beyond place,
and the *now* which is beyond time,
then you will be unable to doubt
your limitless freedom.

180

I am here in service to your freedom.
My whole life is here with you,
waiting for that moment when you hatch
out of the shell of personal identity.

181

We are already nothing,
with the complex of being something.
If only we knew this, our sorrows would be no more.

182

Your drive for freedom will bring up whatever is
hidden within you. Resistances, doubts, egoic
tendencies will come to the surface. Look at them,
and with the skill that you have acquired in satsang,
you will transcend them. You will see them for
what they are, for your eyes see from the true
position. That's all. Now you will come to a clarity.
It may take some time for your mind to stabilise
in the heart's stillness, but this is also a sweetness.

Allow some time for this divine maturing.
It is a great joy.

183

You are not here to cope.
You are not here to survive.
You are here to bear witness to
and shine as the glory of God.

You cannot be a part-time Buddha.
There are no good and bad days in or for the Self.
You will not hold such comparisons as good and bad;
they are not relevant.
Sometimes tears happen, sometimes laughing,
but it is not significant enough to talk about.
The more you keep saying, 'This thing or that thing
happened to me and that person did this to me,'
the more you are fabricating a self
who will suffer its projections.
Your 'person' will perceive others as 'persons' also
and will disturb them by requiring that they
relate to you as a 'person' and not as the Self.
So keep checking in all the time.
This is how you cleanse your being
of the noise of personhood.

185

Both the devil and God are in us.
On one side there is a force
which pulls us towards personhood.
On the other, a power rises towards pure consciousness.
You—whatever that is—must discern what is true.
You who are aware of both extremes, who are you?

Having come so far as to discover all appearances to be
unreal, the final obstacle is the identity of the seeker.
The seeker says, 'I just want to be free, I just want to be
who I am. That is all I want now, nothing else.'
He says, 'Please remove the last obstacle,'
not knowing it is he himself. But all of this has only been
our dream-talking, dream-walking, dream-living.

Now through the Master's guidance and grace one must
twist oneself loose from this conditioned identity as
a seeker by recognising that it too is observable,
and is therefore phenomenal.
The seeker remains dissatisfied and says,
'You never answer my questions.'
The question and the questioner have been answered
but can the 'seeker' accept an answer
that reveals its unreality?
He says, 'Wow, but without me, how can I be found?'
And I say, Without 'you' how can you be lost?
When this is grasped,
one has found the master key to awakening.

Your mind is like a tree with all its leaves,
practising to be still in a windy place.

You are pure awareness.
You are not awareness sometimes
and sometimes not awareness.
The idea that you are only
sometimes awareness
and sometimes not awareness
is itself an idea appearing in awareness.
Be aware of this.

189

It's not important that you always understand me.
Such expectations limit one's capacity
to grasp great things instantly.
Within the grace of Yes,
all things find their equilibrium
inside the Being spontaneously.

190

If you conquer your person,
you conquer the whole world.

191

Real surrender is when that which you most treasure
is offered wholeheartedly to the Infinite.
Include yourself in this offering.

192

If consciousness had no use for it, it wouldn't happen.

If you imagine the most perfect self you can be,
you could only imagine that because God
gives you that creative power.
But God doesn't have to remember or imagine anything.
People don't realise what love really is.
You say that God is love and love is God,
but you have no idea what it is.
True love is so far away from the limited field
of interrelated opposites, from good and evil,
you and me, this and that, heaven and hell,
right and wrong, and life and death.
Love transcends all.

There is a time when all of these things
become nothing. Nothing at all.
When you realise this,
you automatically know you are inside God
and God is inside you.
You will laugh and laugh and laugh,
or cry and cry and cry,
but all the while,
you are there quietly watching,
like a camera without film,
beyond knowledge or perplexity.

This laughing and crying
needs no reason or explanation.
It is just the spontaneous utterance of freedom
in its most eloquent expression.

If my words are true,
it is you who make them true.
They come alive inside you
because you listen inside your heart.
Not just the words, but what they point to
somehow recognises itself,
and the stagnant, the suppressed,
vanishes in the light of real seeing.
The serpent mind loses its tongue
in the presence of the real Self.
You are the Self.

We are divine beings in a state of recovery,
re-discovering our divinity,
winning back ourselves from the deluded mind.
However, the mind is very much a key player
in the drama called life, because without it,
the consciousness cannot experience transcendence.
And transcendence is the whole purpose of the game.
It is a kingly game when seen
with eyes of understanding.
If you stay stuck in personhood, life will kick your ass.
But if you are open to Truth, then you are continuously
expanding into greater and greater seeing.
Finally, you will say, 'I love this climbing over myself,
this walking through myself into my Self.'

196

Emptiness is the vastest kingdom, rarely discovered,
and yet it is the greatest resting place for all beings.

197

Satsang is here to wash off the mind's face
and to reveal the timeless face of God.

198

Truth is eternally here.
The question is whether the one
who is having any doubt about this, is here.

199

Go for the greater, and the lesser will be taken
care of. Don't worry. Life is not a puzzle.
It is the ego that gets puzzled.
You don't have to work things out.
Simply keep quiet and let it all unfold.
If you think you can work life out,
you create an identity as a solver of life. Big trouble!

Nobody can work it out. It is not to be worked out.
As one surrenders one's ego,
one automatically comes into harmony with life.
Watch as life takes care of life.
It flows spontaneously and perfectly in each form.
Let go to the dance of existence.
Why miss the best show on earth?

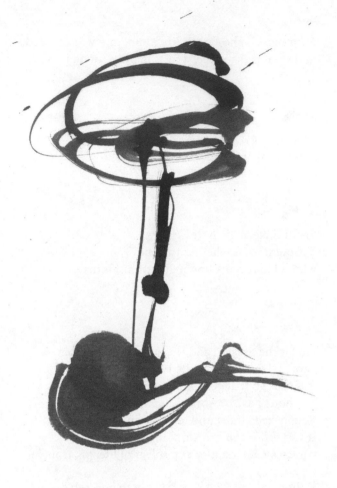

200

A true meeting of the Heart is like
water being poured into water.
Neither division nor separation is there.
When one finds the Truth,
neither the seeker nor the finder remain.
Whose discovery is this?

Your urge to control life controls you.

Love does not need an intention or object to love.
It is the highest expression of the being
in recognition of itself.
It is the unity of being.
Like the fragrance and the flower are one,
your being radiates this love—effortlessly.
You are the Self.
Silence, wisdom and joy are your perfume.
It is here when you leave your luggage outside.
Luggage means identity, desire, memory, projections
—who you think you are and who you want to be.
This beauty awakens in you
when there is space for the beautiful One.
Surrender.
Be entirely empty of 'you'.
And the One alone shines in that space, timelessly.

203

There is no standard for one who is liberated. You
neither have to give all your things away nor live naked
in some cave. Truth is not like that. Each expression
is unique. A liberated being may have a hundred
houses, yet they don't pursue wealth. Another is
without possessions and with no care in the world.
Both these beings are equally free and equally happy,
not being enslaved by the things of this world.

The real is not an effect. It is not bubbly.
The real is not anything where you can say,
'Wow! This is it!'
Perhaps such phenomena are pleasant,
but they are not the absolute.
Don't be looking for blissful states.
Though they may come,
they are as momentary as
beautiful clouds passing in the sky.
There is a bliss beyond bliss—unfading, timeless, whole.
Here, you are home.
The space of beingness is your house.
You have crossed over from death to life.

What is most beautiful
is when a human is being undone as an ego,
when the belief in a personal self is merging
with its own source—the universal Being.
When the tribal is absorbed in the universal,
the human being has moved from person
to pure presence and is in harmony.
This is the real yoga.
Every person belongs to some tribe
—a tribe shaped by personal identity and conditioning.
But the universal mind transcends the tribal mind.
On the surface, such a one may appear
to belong to some tribe
but internally they are the universal Self.

206

At a certain point, one comes to see,
Oh my God I am cherishing so many lies!
But still you continue to hold onto these imaginings
because you feel you will not be yourself without them,
whereas in fact, you will not be your Self with them.

207

Do not cling to any concept
or belief of how life should be,
for you will be radiant
when your projections
are unfolding favourably
but when they are not,
you will crumble.

When you are empty, it does not hurt if you have to
suddenly change direction in life. Like when a fly has
to change direction, it does not deliberate nor complain.
Everything is a spontaneity. It can fly in any direction.
That's why it's called a 'fly'. Left, right, upside down,
diagonal—anywhere is good. If something that you
intend to happen does not happen, and you have to
change direction, your intention should not be so
intense that you suffer disappointment. A free mind
does not rely on any phenomenal outcome. To have
investments in phenomenality is setting yourself up
for trouble. And yet everything is inside the great play
of consciousness. What cannot be inside the great
play? Every movement is in the great play. Even the
players not believing in the play, or the creator of the
great play, are inescapably part of the great play.

Can you imagine meeting with God and knowing there
is nothing you could say that would make him upset
with you? And when you know you cannot do anything
to change this love for you, then many suppressed
feelings just leave you. Nothing to be offended, nothing
to judge, nothing to forgive nor to heal. Nothing
has ever been remembered of anything wrong you
think you ever did. I tell you that you don't have to
imagine this, because it is true. People worry and say,
'Man, you really don't know what kind of thoughts I
have.' They are only terrible because you think they
are yours and that there is a 'you' who thinks them.

210

As long as there is wanting in you,
especially for someone or something
to make you happy,
paradoxically, this is a sure way
to make yourself feel lacking
and therefore miserable.

211

Nothingness does not remove anything at all.
It neither attains nor transcends anything.
Nothingness is not affected or intimidated by anything.
It neither requires nor depends on anything.
It simply is.
Being complete, it lacks nothing.
Therefore, nothing is required for Nothing to be.
Discovering oneself to be Nothing, this is freedom.

212

There is a silence that is totally impersonal.
It is not the fruit of anybody's work.
Peace is there, but there is no peacekeeper.
This peace is only known
when the noise of the person is not present.
Without the 'person' all that remains is the ever pure.
The ultimate is nobody's achievement at all.

Seeking is the bait.
The seeker is the trap.
The sought is the seeker.
The sought, the seeking and the seeker are one.
That which perceives sought, seeking and seeker
is alone the Real.

Be inside the inside itself.
Don't hold this thought that you are journeying
towards something, because that itself
is a belief leading to unnecessary despair.
What you are searching for is already what you are.

I do not know anything. I do not know anyone.
There is just this unfading joy dancing inside my heart
whenever I see a human being set free
from the delusion of ego
and expressing gratitude
to the Supreme.

Awakened beings are always on the planet.
It is not mere books that will give you conviction.
It is to encounter one whose life is the evidence of Truth.
A primal knowing within us recognises such a one.
Seek out and cherish such company.

217

Remaining as awareness, delusions fall away
and mind returns to its natural abode, the Heart.
Do not fight any tendency.
Simply stay as the detached witness
who is ever present and without form.
Follow this advice.
It works.

218

I'm not telling people things to help them.
I'm telling them things to kill this sense of separation
which is the cause of all trouble
—to kill the womb that keeps on giving birth to egos.
This is the love I have in my heart.

219

Don't start out on any path before first finding out
where you are starting from and who you actually are
—the one about to start a journey.
Don't make tattoos out of any teaching
or fall in love with the finger pointing to the sun
and so miss the real goal.
All real pointers lead you back to your own Self.

220

That which witnesses this,
but itself is not this,
That is also this.

221

Wherever you find yourself,
right there is a door to your inmost Being.
But usually there is a crowd around this door.
They have set up a fish market at the gate of Heaven,
'We have nice fish for you, the best you'll taste . . .'
and instead of going through,
you're smelling the fish,
and you are smelling of fish!

When the moment of truth comes,
the mind is making up excuses.
One day you will have to give up your stories and admit,
'I have no accomplice, all this play is Me alone.'

222

When one is without ego, one becomes immediately
free of all personal judgements and perceives
life and the world with divine eyes and mind.
Nothing is offensive to such a one, and they
remain in perfect serenity and peace always.

223

If every book on spirituality
brought about one awakening,
the world would be rich with Buddhas.
But where the hell are they?

224

People say, 'I can't do it. I can't do it.'
I'm not asking you to do it.
I'm asking you to see.

225

The nature of any illusion is that when it is seen
clearly, it loses its power. You can never lose yourself.
Everything else you may lose, but you cannot lose your
true Self, because it alone is real. The person is only
a t-shirt worn by the Infinite for a moment or two.

226

O Supreme One,
Even to look into the mirror of self-inquiry
is impossible without your grace, O unfathomable One.
O pure and perfect Shiva, awareness Supreme,
dispel now any remaining delusion here.

227

Time is the space for the 'person'
who is nothing other than mind ticking away.
Timelessness is the space of the Self.

228

Beloved, please listen:
It is not wise to compare your life to that of others, for
each life stream is unique and is the expression of pure
spirit and being. Know within your heart that your life
is tailor-made for awakening in response to the will
of the Supreme Being. Even if great hardship comes
your way, don't complain, judge or fall into self-pity.
Don't waste energy like this. Rather, use these same
difficulties and circumstances to sharpen your powers
of discernment and to intensify your drive for liberation
and freedom from all psychological conditioning and
evil forces. You are here as life itself flowing towards
its own divine source. Regard your life as auspicious.

229

Be fully in your heart.
Otherwise whatever you do
will be merely average or, at best, impressive
—not miraculous, not magnificent.
Only when you commit or surrender with all your heart
will you enter the realm of the divine.

230

Imagining yourself to be the body,
no wonder you have all these ailments.
Imagining yourself to be the mind,
no wonder you have all these worries.
Knowing yourself to be consciousness,
no wonder there is all this space and peace.
Realising you are the unborn awareness,
no wonder you are supremely happy.

The greatest disciples of a master like Christ were not
necessarily his contemporaries. They may not have
been among the renowned twelve. The twelve had to
be who they were for the story to bring about what it
should according to God's will. But the best disciples
may not have been there at the actual time of the
historical Christ. It is the total trust and belief in the
power of his words and spirit that produces a true
disciple. 'The best one' means one who disappears
in the Master due to perfect understanding and
surrender—one in whom the concept of separation
has perished. Perhaps his greatest disciples are yet
to be born, and through them he will come again.

Nothing is required of you.
Only when you are a person do you need to prove
something—to feel worthy, interesting or special.
Why this haemorrhaging of energy trying to be
special when you can simply be yourself?

Only when a human being becomes empty of ego
is it transformed into
a divine manifestation of the Supreme.
When there is sufficient space made through
the absence of the 'person', then the divine cannot hide.
It must reveal itself as the Lord inside that form.

If someone knew the winning lottery numbers,
would you not make sure that you knew them also?
Once known, would you not ensure
that you have the ticket and the receipt?
Why not have a similar attitude for the Truth?
I am giving you the lottery number for freedom.
I am openly showing everyone right now,
This is the way, keep it inside your heart.
Don't say, 'But I need a private meeting with you
so you can personally tell me as well.'
We are listening too personally,
like your individuality matters so much.
But you must listen universally.
If you want to meet with the Master,
you must be willing to meet on his terms, not yours.
Forget your insecurities ... your private meeting
may have to take place in front of everybody.
Whatever the Master says to one,
he says to all who have the thirst for his guidance.
Drink in these words.

First you must come to recognise presence.
That which is aware of both presence and absence
is beyond them both.
You don't have to talk about these things.
If you were struck down and couldn't speak another
word, the Truth would still be alive in you.
That which I point to,
none can alter or remove.

The mind is apparently making someone's life hell
and you call this someone you.
This 'you' who is suffering from the mind
is now trying to go beyond the mind.
It says, 'Mooji, help me to make this leap.'
But to make this leap is just another thought
arising in that which is already beyond the mind.
Now, become aware of the power of presence
which is unaffected by the mind-play.
Don't miss my pointing. Go directly to this awareness
space, for right there is where all the mind's cunning
plays are exposed as mere imagination.
Just be there.
It does not suffer, nor can it be attacked by thoughts.
It is immaculate—untouched.
Yourself and it are one. Confirm this.
It is the sage's abode.

The whole world has got it wrong.
You think you did something wrong
and you have spent so much time trying to correct it.
Yet somehow all of this is in the mind of God,
who creates all this potential,
creates all these colours and paints all these pictures.
Somehow there is a place for every stroke.
You, consciousness, are God's paintbrush.
The world is your canvas.
You are also his living work of art.
Delight in the knowing of this.

Even after awakening to one's real nature,
some habits may still appear to be playing out,
but their effects are gradually
being thinned out
through the grace of the Self.
Your inner being knows, somehow,
that despite all of this fluctuation,
all is well within the grand functioning.
It intuitively knows all is a passing show.
The old tendencies are being spring-cleaned out,
leaving one in a state of serene neutrality and joy.
And therein lies one's unfading happiness.
Even when the body is sick,
one remains in the undisturbed state of the Self.
You are waltzing with the Supreme
but there is no 'two',
no separation, just a wholeness.

The world that is conceived in the minds of men
has to fail so that the human being can aspire
for what is everlasting and true.
Whether the world comes to an end or not
is not at the mercy of men.
Find that in yourself which is pure and unchanging.
All that you really seek is there.
Don't waste time on other things,
about what the world looks like,
what's going to happen in the future.
These things just trouble your mind
and make it very busy and incapable of inner focus.
So leave all that for a moment.
Where help can be offered you will know,
'It is my time to act.'
To be an instrument of God
you have to become completely empty of 'you'.

When you are sufficiently empty, you become
a perfect vessel for the manifestation
and embodiment of His grace.
But while you are still nurturing your identity,
the light has no chance.
You tell me, 'Until I am there, show me what to do now.'
I say, No, because then I am colluding with you
to cheat you out of your timelessness.
And this I cannot do.
I don't want you to cheat yourself.
The solution to all sorrows is ever present,
but something is turning away from this chance.
Don't trust in that.
A single liberated being sheds enough light
to raise the consciousness of many.
Who is that one?
Could it not be you.

How can I call that which is without form beautiful?
That which gives beauty to beauty, life to life.

This radiant joy, this profound silence,
this immense emptiness is like solid ether
when experienced inside a body.
Here, immeasurable silence, unmatched beauty,
unbroken peace, unfading love, shine timelessly.

Mooji on Arunachala, February 1994

Intimate moments

Mahasamadhi Day of Mooji's mother, Euphemia, in the Shiva Temple, Monte Sahaja 2015

The Sword of Truth

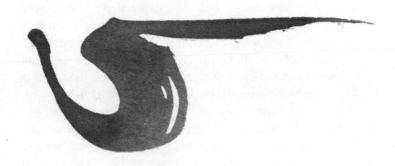

The mind, the illusory person, doesn't want to change. It is very afraid of change. It doesn't mind praying for change in the world, but doesn't want to change itself. The mind doesn't mind playing at spirituality. It doesn't mind meeting God, even meeting Him as an equal, but it doesn't want to exchange itself for God. The psychological mind is the devil actually—but not totally, because it is mixed with the beingness. The mind wants to sell you a brand of spirituality which builds your ego, telling you, 'Yes, let's do these exercises of embracing each other and praying for the world,' but these things do not challenge you.

When the time comes to be deeply challenged about your identity and who you are, all the fears and resistances come, and you start to feel like you are crumbling. Actually, you are not crumbling. Just the false skin is crumbling. And in the beginning, it's not even crumbling, but just threatened. When the mind is threatened, it is going to fight to not crumble—and it's a nasty player. It will bring up any doubt that it can find from wherever it can find it. It will look for your Achilles' heel to try and puncture your resolve so that it can drive you again into the pit of personal identification, distraction and delusion.

I am here to encourage you. Don't panic. Don't be weak. Now is the time to be strong. You are stronger than you think, but you are strongest when you remember and draw upon the power of God. Grace is with you, but you must turn your face towards Grace and not towards your mind, for that is dis-grace. Know that everything is on your side, but you must fight for yourself. Don't give up. If you give up, not even God can help you. Everything is here to encourage and support your victory. Come, come. Stand up. Why? Because to live, you must stand up! You are not a snake. If He wanted you to be a snake, He wouldn't give you limbs. He would say, 'Wriggle.' But He gave you limbs—limbs of the Spirit—to stand up, because when you stand up in the power of God, you can fight anything. You can overcome the world.

I want to see that people reach deep into themselves, behind the facade of the person, and find the presence of God within. I want to see that people blow away these miserable states and live this life as the living Truth itself. You may think we are suffering from conflict, wars, famines and droughts. But no, we are suffering from ego! The ego is the atomic bomb that we drop on ourselves, in a way. Why do I say that? Because we are not helpless. As a person you are pretty much helpless, but you are powerful as Being. The change that really has to happen in the human kingdom is not a more advanced technological change, advancing in the outer things. We must be advanced in the inner world and rise above shallow, fleshly ambitions, to find again our original nature.

All this play is in the world—but the sword of Truth is also here. The whole thing, from start to finish, is illusion. 'This life I'm living, my family, my attachments, my hopes for the future, trying to save the planet and what religion I am' is all a big, big dream. Even myself standing here talking is in the dream—but I'm awake. When you are awake, it is very different. You don't panic. You don't run. You don't hide under the bed or under a rock, because wherever you are, you know God is right here. This is not fantasy at all. Does fear come in this body? Yes, it comes, but it cannot proliferate. It cannot grow. Human feelings come in consciousness, but they are seen immediately and can never overtake. This is a very important thing.

Knowing the seeming power of delusion, I feel for all beings. My strength is that I know always that it is just an illusion. I have broken the mind, because I see whatever is appearing is just an illusion. It is all passing, you see, and nothing can stand up against the might of this seeing. Whatever it is, I know it is phenomenal. No matter what form it takes, it is phenomenal. When you come to the power of this conviction, you too are not going to be broken.

Mine is not so much a life in the world,
but a life in the spirit;
the bright and innermost Being.

I am the womb of life
—perfect reality, timeless Truth.

242

The question 'Who am I?' is the most important
question a human being can ask. To feel some attraction
to this question already signals an auspicious life. From
the birth of this body something inside has been saying,
'I am, I want, I know, I love, this is me, this is mine,'
but when asked, What or who is this 'me' or 'I'?
no clear answer is given or formed.
The 'I' itself appears to know many things
but it doesn't know its own Self.
What exactly arises as 'I'?
What is the substance of 'I'?
These are the most powerful questions
that can emerge inside the human consciousness.
Why powerful?
Because they break open and dispel every
delusion and so remove the ego's grip on us.

Ego is the unreal identity and nature that makes us
feel uneasy in the presence of other beings. It often
brings fear and insecurity which causes us to hold
onto feelings of rejection, jealousy, hatred and desire.

However, by its very nature, ego can also help us
to grow in understanding and aspire for lasting
freedom by forcing us to seek what is true within
ourselves. Satsang speeds up our liberation.

243

The one who starts the inquiry into the
nature of the Self will not finish the inquiry,
but will be finished by the inquiry!

244

What you are seeing is the dance of transience.
Everything comes and goes,
but there is something that does not come and go.
It is pure, unchanging awareness.
And it is what every living being is.
You are not your self-image.
Sometimes the mind comes and says,
'Awareness comes and goes,'
but what would witness awareness coming and going?
Another awareness? There are not two awarenesses.
The thought 'awareness comes and goes'
is itself a thought arising in the single and
unchanging awareness you already are.
Be clear about this and the whole forest of noise
is going to be burnt down.

245

The Self has no doubt about itself. It is not confused.
It is absolutely what you are. But relatively what you
are is the one seeking it. Now, you can look from your
relative standpoint, but is your relative standpoint
not seen from your absolute standpoint? Judge which
is the greater and confirm your true position.

246

Why would you exchange the most holy thing for the
most mundane things, and thus accept the unreal when
the real—God himself—is sitting inside your heart?

You are called in this life to come home to your Self. Not home to somewhere else; home is never somewhere else. You are returning to your own being by the only gracious power in the world, and you are afraid it won't take care of your life. This is called ignorance and suffering. You prioritise your projections, thinking that somehow if you surrender to that power, it may not give you what you want—as though what you want could be greater than what it would reveal in you. It seems ridiculous when it is put like this, but some force is inside making us think, 'If I had a chance to run the world or let God continue running it, I think I could do a better job.' You wouldn't say this, of course. You don't know how to put things right. In fact, nothing is wrong if you have the right mind. You see wrong because something inside is not functioning harmoniously. That same thing wants to run away from home, and you are taking sides with it. Remember, the thing you are running away *with* is the very thing you should be running away *from*.

Upon discovering Truth,
the natural love one has for oneself
expands until it encompasses the whole world.
This love erases ego.

249

There is always a part of our mind that wants to tame people so that they don't threaten us. And we play the game to be nice, to be cute, to be attractive, funny or entertaining, because we are uncomfortable with the sense of 'other'. The Master is neither 'other' nor 'another'. Suddenly it is you who feels like the 'other'. When you encounter the presence that you cannot impress, inspire or manipulate, then all kinds of insecurities come to the surface to be burnt.

This is the greatness of the Master.
Let the Master be your white fire.

250

Sometimes we try to give birth to the Self with the mind when the mind is the very child of the Self.

251

Aspiration has to be a part of the drama of realisation. In the beginning, something has to search.
You have to long for something. Before you had this longing, you knew nothing at all. You were in ignorance. You were not free. You needed to fake-learn something only to get rid of this learning once true understanding is revealed—and yet none of it is a waste of time. Sometimes consciousness creates the sense of a problem in order to experience transcending it. This is the game of life. You are the timeless experiencing the sense of time. How strange that time is needed to discover the timeless.

There is going to come a time when you will say,

I once believed that everyone had to like me,
but now this belief is no more.
I once believed I had to be the best person
I could be in order to be free, but no more.
I once believed that I had to first do everything
I needed to do in the world,
and only when I had done that and I was satisfied
could I turn my attention to Self-discovery.
I once believed that.
I once believed that it was up to someone else
to make me happy.
That seems a long time ago.
I once believed that I was not worthy,
but I see now that was nonsense.
I once believed I was not ready,
but I see now it's not true.
I once believed that I had to practise more,
meditate longer, be more sincere,
but I saw it's not like that.
Life is not so strenuous or cruel.
I believed so many things that were not true.
Then I realised nothing obstructs the freedom I am.

253

You have to be clear of your right position.
When we are speaking from duality,
we refer to ourselves as personalities,
as individuals, as ego—the mind.
And mind is never totally happy where it is.
It hitchhikes from one place to another,
from one state to another.
When it's not happy with the present, it goes to the past.
When it's not happy with the past, it projects a future.
It is never content with anything.
The belly of the mind is never full.

254

When everything is given up, You are found.

255

To clean your person is like trying to clean a garbage bag.
Why are you wasting time when eventually
you are going to throw the garbage and the bag away?

256

The intellect of the human being is a very tiny thing
and totally inadequate as an instrument
for comprehending the might of the universe.

Don't try to become a Buddha.
Just be yourself.
That is the Buddha.

After the realisation of the Self, you are not
necessarily just going to sit around doing nothing.
Of course, this could also happen, but you may
even find yourself more active than before while
retaining full energy, and yet internally there is total
serenity, unbroken peace, a clear and empty mind.
A mighty presence prevails. None can explain.

Don't judge or try to measure the Self by activity.
Someone's life could appear full of activity, but all
of it is springing from tremendous peace. They don't
claim any word or any action. Everything is just
arising spontaneously out of the life force. Whether
active or still, the Self is the guru of each expression.
None can fathom its ways. The only way to fathom
is to drop the mind and the sense of a personal self.

Just be empty, and all this you will spontaneously know.

259

Sometimes you think you have to go outward to become universal. No. As we bring our attention inside the heart, something becomes singular—non-dual. Paradoxically, this singularity and universality are one.

260

The ego says, 'Truthfully, this is what I believe.'
But the ego itself is a lie.

261

Open your windows. Open your doors.
Open your mind, your eyes and your heart to Truth.
Trust in and be one with the Supreme Being.

262

Many spiritual and religious practices focus on uplifting the personal self, whereas self-inquiry quickly exposes the person as limited and false so that further time is not wasted on continuing a ghost story. One's attention can then rest joyfully inside the natural Heart-Self.

263
Trying to stop the mind is like
trying to stop the wind, dressed as a kite.

264

Throw off the conviction that you are bound.
In fact, you can also throw the belief that you are free,
for that which truly exists is beyond
even conviction and belief.
It simply is.
Not holding onto anything,
including the sense 'I am',
what remains?
Please share your findings.

265

People don't change people.
Grace changes people into presence.

266

You say, 'I know I am That.'
And now something is saying,
'But it is mind that knows that.'
But what knows that the mind knows that?
Contemplate this.
Is this too subtle a question to put to you now?
Someone will grasp this and recognise
the unchanging awareness that is ever present.
Something may be avoiding such clarity,
such direct pointing.
The Truth always seems inconvenient
from the position of the lie.

267

You are waiting for God
because you are waiting for 'other'.
But he is never showing up.
If you are not looking for God as 'other',
then what do you see?
Stop putting God in the 'other' place.
And now where is God?
Mind cannot breathe here.
It needs to go to 'other',
for the sense of other sustains mind.
Mind cannot see God and live as mind,
therefore mind makes a caricature of him.
Him is not him. Him is not her.
Him is not 'you' as you.
If you take yourself to be a person, you also are 'other'.
Don't touch 'other' and there is no problem.
Don't touch 'other' and there is no time.
There is neither separation nor union in the Truth.
Why should there be union
when separation never happened?
I don't know who hears my words.
I have been waiting to say them.
Maybe tonight God wants to hear.
Maybe God has been satisfied with the play
of 'I' and 'other' for a while but tonight he says,
'I have had enough of that game.
There are no 'others' now.'
You try and figure out the rest.

I am not touched by 'bad' things happening.
I am touched by expressions of kindness,
selflessness and openness.
I am touched by acts of faith, trust and courage
which spring from an egoless heart.
I am touched by the light, wisdom and presence of
God shining out of the heart, mind and body
of living beings devoted to Truth.
I am not touched by the devil.
I am touched by God
and the living company
of the seekers of Truth.

Suffering comes because of an earlier mistake:
we don't know who we are.

When life exposes your hidden flaws,
avoid identifying with the reflex
to defend or protect them.
Instead, open your heart to the possibility
of transformation and transcendence
by saying Yes inside your being.
Fall fully into the embrace
of the Lord within.

The one who is free of every and any intention,
even the intention to be free, is free indeed.

272

If today was your last day in this body,
would the opinions of your mind make any difference to you?
Why not then live like this?

273

The Truth cannot be developed.
It can only be discovered.
The Self has nowhere to go
while you are being the 'non-Self'.
It doesn't say, 'Well, I'll just wait over there
with the others until you find me.' No.
Without the Self, even your mistaken identity
as a person could not be.
Are you not always your Self?

274

If you know many things but your Self
you don't know, how reliable is your knowledge?

275

When you come to the state of presence, naturally
you are in a much lighter state. And there is definitely a
distaste at the thought of going back to the state of
personhood. Despite that, you may experience the
sense of swinging into the state of personhood from
time to time. But it becomes increasingly unbearable.
It may even seem that you suffer more than before,
but it is only because you now know a higher state
of being and this makes all lower states intolerable.
And this is good. It instils and strengthens
the aspiration to be free.
Don't be discouraged.
Everything is serving your awakening.
And if you are genuinely seeking Truth,
you will be carried along
even while you are in this state of identity.
The support is there until the very end of delusion.
Keep this in your mind and heart.

276

If you really want to know me, then stop focusing
on other things for a moment and find that which
cannot change within yourself. I am there. I am the
unchanging one reflecting your own immutable Self.

277

You can only suffer from thought
if you yourself are a thought.

278

Do not allow your mind to become so easily disturbed
by the fleeting soap-bubble experiences of this world.
Know your mind's essence to be imperishable,
indivisible and unborn.
Without your Self, nothing is,
for things cannot be their own witness.
It is in the light of sentience that the world is seen.
You are not an object.
All phenomena report to the consciousness in you,
the formless Self.
Know your Self to be that in which they arise,
play and are eventually absorbed.

279

When the intellect is present, there is talk of 'I and God'.
When the intellect is itself seen, can the seer be found?

280

God has stolen my mind and left me with nothing
and as nothing that can be fathomed.
Oh, what good fortune!

281

Sometimes, the thing you think is happening is
not the thing that is happening. This is true of
life. Much of what you think life is, is not what it
is. Sometimes you see an action happening and
it's not what is really going on. Other things are
going on that you cannot see. And if you take your
version as real, you will continue disagreeing with
life and having lots of opinions. If you are empty
of opinions, you discover a synchronicity that you
cannot deny. There is a higher power working beyond
and behind the human mind that is coordinating
things beyond our capacity to comprehend as a
person. Live as though it is already your truth.

282

I have neither past, present nor future.
I am Nobody. I am Nothing.
Therefore, as I am, I am supremely happy.

283

Now that joy is arising, do not cling to this joy,
but rather rest in and as that
from which this joy springs.

284

Be your Heart and mind will follow.

When you come to that auspicious point of a
breakthrough into real freedom, the greatest
distractions come. They happen to everybody
—even a Christ or a Buddha. Something has to
be squeezed out from inside. Distractions appear
to shake your house to the foundations, but you will
see the illusoriness of this as you continue standing
in the Supreme. At times like this, you may feel a
wobbling, as does everyone, but by not losing your
ground, they turn out to your advantage.
You must build muscle out of such difficulties.
You have to! There is no other way for a seeker.
Some begin to fade as they get knocked back
a bit. They lose heart quickly. Their courage
withers away in the hot sun of life's trials and
tribulations and they are soon gone.
I say, No! Don't go with that now. Fight through this.
Remember you are not going through these things
—they are going through you.
All things pass, except the Infinite.

As soon as the 'seeker' is seen
to be just a thought
arising in awareness,
he merges into awareness
and the spell of separation is broken.
The seeker doesn't become a finder.
The seeker ceases becoming
and merges into oneness.

287

We are the pure, timeless and unchanging being, but
due to the debilitating effects of the egoic or personal
identity, many people have drifted away from the
natural state and so begin suffering from deep
insecurities within themselves. Consequently, many
human beings want to become 'someone special', and
so much energy goes into this. But in truth, or you may
say from a higher standpoint, no one is special because
to be special requires that others have to be less special.
Maybe there is a sense, 'If I am not different and
special, then I will become vulnerable.' But actually,
to be special, to be anyone, *is* to be vulnerable.
Paradoxically, the way to be free of psychological
vulnerability and the sense of separation is to become
nobody. Somehow, without the attachment and
pride of personal identity, we feel and know, 'I am
the same one in everyone.' The sense of 'I' being one
with 'others' now seems greater and truer than the
sense of 'other' being apart and different from 'I'. We
seem afraid of this discovery yet it is a liberation.
And so much love, real joy and compassion arises.

288

Whatever happens in your head is not you.
Whatever happens in your body is not you.
Whatever happens in the world is not you.
Whatever happens is not you.
Yet none of it can exist without you,
the perceiver of it all.

289

I don't believe what people think and say.
Just be quiet.
When you are quiet,
I believe you.

290

The world is not what you think it is.
The world is exactly what you think it is.
Find the place within you where
both these statements are true.

291

While the sense of duality persists in us,
let us turn our faces inwards
and bow down into the lap of the Supreme One
dwelling inside the heart of every being.
Om Sri Gurudev.

292

Mind arises and assumes the shape of your
hidden tendencies. Mind cannot think.
It is you who think by identifying with thought.
Actually, both mind and the thinker
of thought are thought.
Think about this.

293

I keep pointing you to simply discover your Self.
If something is to be discarded,
it will happen automatically.
You don't have to try to get rid of anything
—just discover what is true. That is all.
If you feel you have to get rid of something,
you put another condition in front of yourself:
'When I get rid of this, then I will be closer to my goal.'
All these are forms of postponement
in the guise of Self-discovery.
The mind feeds on this 'when and then', 'if and but'.
All this is not needed to discover the Truth.

294

Be nobody.
When you are somebody, there are so many duties
that even to be yourself is such a hassle.
When you are nobody, you escape from every trap.
It is immediate freedom!

295

Don't study. If it happens, let it happen.
But don't be dedicated to study.
Be dedicated to drowning yourself,
to disappear, to vanish in the absolute Self.
With such an attitude
one moves from death to everlasting life.

There must always be some distance between you
and the phenomena that you perceive.
When you are more aware of your Self
than you are of the world,
then somehow you have crossed over.
When you are more aware
of your personal self and the world
rather than your awareness Self,
then you are still in exile.
When you are anchored in the Self,
there is a vibration there.
It is like you are insulated
from the impact of worldly functioning,
vaccinated against worldly delusions.
Something is just not touched.
Touched, yet untouched.
Affected, yet unaffected.
Immaculate being.

The Self is always one and unchanging.
It cannot move to somewhere else,
for it is everywhere present and the same.
It cannot be hidden by something called mind,
because the mind is of the Self.
Where is the problem?

298

When I look inside, it all seems a mess.

You have no inside and also you have no outside.
Now live as what remains.

299

The ego is meant to be there because without it, there would
be no such thing as transcendence of ego. Within the
play, *maya* is needed for there to be Self-realisation.
And if there was no ego to transcend, there could never
have been a Christ, or a Buddha, or a Mohammed, or
a Ramana Maharshi or an Anandamayi Ma.
They represent transcendence over ego.

300

There is no 'other'.
The truth is that you are always alone.
Even when you are with others,
you are essentially alone. However, it is a beautiful
aloneness; it is not psychological.
You are not alone anymore as a person.
You are alone as everything—as the only One.
All the various 'others' are only forms of the single Self.

301

Satsang is tenderising your being. We have grown a bit of outer
skin, a bit of toughness, and in satsang you are being tenderised
again. You are becoming much more sensitive, more open and
child-like. With this renewed receptivity and flexibility, your
true powers can flow again. If you are tough, it means you
have swallowed the person somehow. The person is a very
tough thing. Nothing can digest it; it can only be spat out.
Only then will everything flow beautifully again.

If some heavenly being appeared who possessed the
power to grant you either all the knowledge in the
world or instead make you completely empty of worldly
knowledge but full of the pure wisdom of the Self,
which would you choose?
Well actually, it would be meaningless to offer
you emptiness if you don't already have a sense
of what this is, you see. It will not be attractive
to your worldly or conditioned mind.
For the conditioned human mind, knowledge is far
more appealing than emptiness. Therefore, it is only
as you begin discovering the magnificence, peace and
joy of emptiness that it will hold any attraction for
you. The emptiness that I speak about, or rather point
towards, is the same as the true Heart of the universe.
Only after you have tasted your own emptiness,
your own true nature and Self,
will you exclaim, 'Oh, my God.
Awesome.'

The same oneness is manifesting in all.
In all beings, all religions, all expressions,
the same one alone is.
Anyone who has delved inside
—inside the inside itself—
knows God as pure reality
and unfading bliss.
Listen to them as they tell you,
'I am the same one everywhere.
Merge in me.'

304

Do not try to stop any movement,
any sensation, any thought.
Let them flow by.
There is no need to be concerned about these,
simply you are here as pure awareness.
Notice the attention;
if there is any movement to go out, or even in,
it is only another sensation.
There is neither in nor out for you,
there are no measurements for awareness.
Stay as the awareness alone.

305

Mooji, I want to do God's will.
How can I serve God and do his will?

First you must empty yourself of your own will, and
then God can enter and flow through you as your own
natural existence. Know this: the one who is empty of
the sense of personal will finds God everywhere.

306

Every now and then, life causes you to lose your phone,
lose your job, lose your relationship, the things you
think are important, so you can see that you have a
full life independent of them. There are many things
you feel are so essential, but without them, you find
you still have your Self, which is more than all of
them put together. You cannot lose your Self.
This is the most important thing.

Almost everyone who is introduced to the method
of self-inquiry goes through a period of what I call
'paranoid inquiry', where one does not know how to
do it and where to stop. You are trying and trying,
asking, 'Who am I? Who am I? Who am I?' but
only mechanically, so it just doesn't seem to lead
anywhere. In fact, you may feel you are going further
and further astray, crazy even, but then somehow,
an unexpected light shines out from nowhere
and mysteriously something begins to happen.

There is a kind of opening from inside and a
new way of being is emerging. Your heart is
expanding with a joy and light and it is as though
understanding becomes natural and effortless.
You find an unknowable movement inside and
many old, tired and stale things are simply falling
away unforced. Something magical seems to
come alive in you and all is happening by itself.

You know, in Jamaica, when we make dreadlocks
in our hair, we keep twisting and twisting, but in
the beginning they simply do not stay. For a while
nothing seems to be happening but you must
just keep twisting and putting some beeswax in
it. Then one day you wake up and it has all come
together by itself, and you say, 'Wow, it just did
it by itself.' Afterwards, the whole process just
continues naturally. Self-inquiry is a bit like this.

308

At any moment, one of these pointings is going to detonate inside you and blow away everything you are cherishing. Not all of them have to, but if one of them detonates, the rest will follow suit all the way down to the end. At any moment, an entire bank account of illusions—gone. And this is what we call giving birth to your Self again. I am your midwife, and satsang is your hospital room.

309

Let the Truth be revealed out of your stillness.
Personal determination, knowledge or force alone
will not produce the desired results.
Keep quiet.

310

Mooji, how can I become nothing?

There is no need to want to become nothing.
You are already nothing. Empty.
It is a beautiful nothing, and complete also.
It is neither a curse nor an insult.
Nothingness is the highest.
It is higher than any concept or goal.
It is higher than anything in the whole world.
The Lord has revealed this inside my heart.
Therefore I am here now, sharing this with you,
who are nothing other than what I am.

In satsang, a melting is taking place.
Something has taken hold of you,
dissolving all delusions from the inside.
At a certain point, you find you are empty of identity.
Now you don't exist as that old picture.
Only the formless Self exists—powerfully!
The person is imaginary.
Only the Self is, and you are That.
A joyful discovery!

I am the great ocean
calling every living being
to rediscover their ocean-self.
Be the mighty sea, not merely a wave,
a lake, a pond or a fish bowl.
You cannot flow this way.
Therefore, be still
and surrender yourself here.

Be willing to be empty, to be nothing.
If you insist on being something
out of fear of being nothing,
you will not be free
—not in this life,
nor in any life.

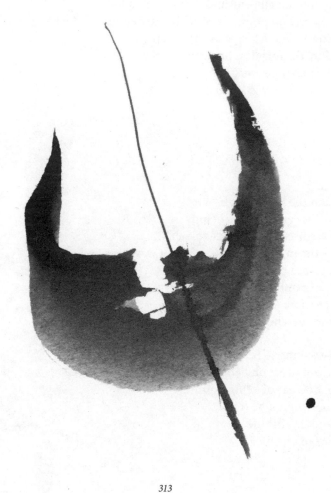

313
There is only one true retreat
and that is to enter this undivided place
where language and the world of meanings cease.

Don't associate any image with your Self.
Go beyond them all.
There is no need to be afraid of thought,
sensation or image.
Simply stay as the awareness.
There is no image of awareness.
Awareness is even more subtle than a feelingless feeling,
one's primal intuition.
You are not separate from That.
You are That.

It is the Supreme Being which is portraying itself
as 'I'-consciousness and person.
How amazing that the single 'I' shines
as ego, as presence and as the Absolute
whilst remaining the immutable one.

I don't know what has caused us to fall asleep,
but I know what makes us wake up.
I know the one who never sleeps.
I watch my sleepful aspect from my unsleeping Self.
I never speak to a mere person.
I only address forms of consciousness.
You are also that consciousness. We are one.
An immense joy and power
is released in that recognition.
Dear one, let Truth confirm itself inside your heart.

317

What is greater:
that there is no more desire
or that there is no more desirer?
Contemplate this.

318

Life flows by itself. How arrogant to think it is you
who makes it flow. Stop interfering and enjoy the ride
of impersonal witnessing.

319

God says 'I am'.
The devil also says 'I am'.
Ego says 'I am'.
And you also say 'I am'.
Will the right 'I am' step forward please.

320

I have nothing to give you
except the authority of my own seeing,
my love and fidelity to Truth.
I speak to you from here.
I have no doubt about you.
Whatever it takes, you have it.

321

Find that which can never come to an end. Time says,
'Everything that is seen, imagined or thought, all of that
belongs to me. I consume every form. All phenomena
dissolve in me. There is only one thing I cannot devour,
and that is pure awareness. I am devoured in that.'

322

Truth touches you and you feel you are falling.
But see how you are falling upwards
into the arms of the Beloved.

323

There is a time when the very longing for Truth
becomes deeply painful, but that pain is a holy
pain. It will burn every other longing. And then
it will bring you to freedom itself. When the pain
of separation becomes unbearable, duality ends.

324

Don't worry about your problems.
Don't worry about the worst thing in the world.
Find the best thing in the world,
and it will take care of everything.
Find the Self.

325

Bear these birth pains.
They are delivering you into ultimate seeing.
Offer no foothold to the illusory mind.
Self is delivering itself to itself
as unborn awareness.

326

Just you offer your existence to existence itself.
Such a request goes very deep
into the heart of the Truth.
When such things are uttered
with any kind of genuineness,
they go into its very soul.
When you give your heart,
you receive your Self.

327

What I speak, let us prove. It is you.
You are the one I come to meet.
Don't let your mind sabotage this opportunity.
You are the one I have come to meet.
Not even to share; just to meet.
You don't have to bring anything.
You don't have to bring flowers or any kind of offering.
Let me meet you as you truly are—you without you.
When will this be?
All my appointments are now.

328

In the midst of the common, the worldly, the mundane,
is the ineffable One. Knowing this, one lives happily
throughout all states. This is the secret that only the
sage knows and enjoys, and reveals to those whose
time has come to flower into divine understanding.

329

If you are looking for an excuse not to find the Truth,
you are on a winning streak all the time because there
are millions of excuses in the mind's playlist. Even
on the path of *Advaita*, which is the most direct way, the
insincere will find clever excuses. In fact, *Advaita* could
be seen to produce the best excuses in the world, such as,
'There is no 'I' existing here or anywhere. Everything is
unreal,' and, 'There is nobody here
to do anything at all, there is only the one Self,'
or, 'Who is to be responsible? In reality nothing
exists.' And from the highest standpoint the words
themselves are true enough, but the speaker is untrue.

There are a lot of these types of behaviours, beliefs,
claims and misconceptions in the 'spiritual'
environment, but it is easy to see if the seeker is
sincere. If you are immersed in genuine inquiry, you
will easily discern whether people are speaking from
direct experience or not. Just the vibration will tell you.
If you are looking for excuses, you cannot come
to the end of opportunities. If you are looking
for Truth, you will expose and discard all excuses
and find the one who cannot be missed.

330

When you meet the Master, he puts a spiritual cowbell
around your neck so that wherever you go, both he
and you know where you each are and so can laugh
together. For when you hear that bell, you are immediately
reminded of your inseparableness from the Master.

331

I am not a library, I am a lighthouse.
You have to attune yourself to my vibration.
Don't bother studying me.
Just tune in and soon you will discover
the vibration of the Self.
To try and study takes a long time.
If you tune in, you actually expand a hundred times faster
than studying, but it requires a trusting and a letting go
—the thing your mind is most afraid of.

332

No one can understand the fire of Grace
nor understand God's cooking
nor that fierce burning deep within.
Let understanding itself be burnt up now.
This is God's fire, and none can put it out.

333

What could possibly be wrong in this moment?
Look inside, outside . . .
what can possibly be wrong
in this moment or any moment
except what you imagine or think?

Mind presents options
Heart offers recognition
Mind imagines
Heart reveals
Mind strays
Heart stays
Mind thinks
Heart knows
Mind is becoming
Heart is being
Mind introduces creature comforts
Heart introduces the Creator

335

At times, you may feel the force of some strong energies arising, but you are still there watching them, aware of their pull. Although such energies are not significant in themselves, they are attractive to the personalised state of consciousness. The true seeker transcends these energies by remaining in the universal being. When consciousness appears as a human being, it takes the *darshan* of duality and goes to sleep in it. As identity it is very difficult to wake up out of that sleep. To awaken to the Self on this planet is auspicious and rare, because the gravity of the senses and the mind are like Gulliver's ropes for the person. The wisdom gained through satsang enables you to burst free from the illusory strength of these ropes. Thereafter, for fun, you may put them around your neck as *malas* to the Supreme.

336

People think they must fight one battle and beat the ego, but you have to fight him until you break his power. It is like weeds. You cannot just pull the weeds up once. They come again and again. You keep pulling them up until you frustrate their power. Then you have some clear space, a lovely season to plant your fruit trees. However, you always keep a watch out. Never think you have beaten the weeds. Just enjoy your space in the here and now. If the weeds return, uprooting them is easy for you. Just don't let a weed become a bush, and a bush a mighty tree.

337

At a higher level of perceiving,
none of this matters at all, at all, at all.
You come to a point where nothing matters at all!
Nothing, nothing, nothing! And all is perfection only.

338

It is pure imagination
to think things won't get done without you.
In real time with the universe,
unexpected forces come to assist
the fulfilment of things which are destined to happen.
The person is like an appendix, a fake organ.
It's there, but nobody really knows what it's there for.

339

The consciousness has painted a self-portrait of itself
as a person and has fallen in love with its own work
of art. And now it's time for the person to go or to
be looked at, and it may seem as if the person wants
to stay, but actually the person does not exist! The
thing is, we don't know that. We say, 'Haha. Oh,
yes, it doesn't exist,' but in your heart you deny it.

Something has been mixed together, like a mixture
of sand and sugar. We don't know which is
which anymore. Satsang intensifies your powers
of discernment so that like a wise ant you will
take the sugar and leave the sand untouched.

340

How paradoxical, we learn so much only to become limited. We study, study, study to learn all these things, but your very knowledge turns you into a fool because you become so narrow. You lose the natural flexibility of your mind to comprehend all manner of things. This learned mind has been shaped into a groove—you become a groovy fool. It's like you buy a fishing rod and go out to sea, but instead of catching a fish, you find a snake on the end of your line. You take your fishing kit back to the shop and complain, 'It doesn't work. I caught a snake instead of a fish.' How strange it is that the learned fool imagines himself superior. Such is the foolishness of conditioned learning.

341

Mooji, sometimes it feels like you're beating the shit out of us.

If I don't beat the shit out of you,
it will just become compost
for your ego-mind.

I cannot relate to you as if you are someone with a problem. That's just too much of a miserable state for me. If I do, I actually reinforce and perpetuate an identity in you that causes you continuous suffering. Nobody should want to go there with you. Only by not supporting your delusion will you hopefully come out of it. But I cannot guarantee this.

Why this loyalty to your time-bound identity when you could remain joyfully in your timelessness?

If your master relates to you on the level of delusion, you are in master-trouble!

Why do you keep God as 'other'?
It is like you are always saying,
'God, stay over there and don't disturb me
while I practise to get back to you.'
But he is always here!
'Yes, yes!' you say, 'I know this intellectually
but what is the best mantra to get directly to you?'
'But I am you,' he says.
'I am you,' you say.
'That sounds nice. I am you, I am you, I am you . . .'
And while you are busy chanting,
you miss God who is inseparably here.
That's exactly what we are doing!

Don't be in front of the mind. Be behind the mind.
Then you can observe the mind—if you even care to.
As soon as it becomes clear to you
that you are outside the bubble of the mind play,
you are immediately in a different atmosphere.
You are in the atmosphere of the Self and far too joyful
to be bothered by as small a thing as the mind.

345

My Father is the source of all. Trust in him.
Offer yourself up fully to his grace.
This is the way to liberation.

346

All this life, all that you see through the senses and
the mind, is all the Self. This daily life that we all
perceive, it is all the Self. There is no need to turn
away from it. Only see it with all-encompassing eyes.
Say, 'Even if time will dissolve all things visible, time
is still only a power inside myself—the timeless one.'

Awareness can never be an object. It cannot be
perceived phenomenally. Being consciously conscious
of awareness is an action you cannot do! Insight
is simply opening up. What you are searching for
has already happened. Actually it didn't happen.
It is before all happening. It is already so. But there
is some movement being believed in that says, 'I
still don't get it.' You will come to see that the
'I' that needed to 'get it' w.as itself the apparent
obstacle because it created a sense of separation.

I am using concepts in order to remove your concepts,
and when both my concepts and your concepts are
nullified, then what remains is already here now,
closer than contact, closer than intimacy. In fact, it
is not even intimate, for intimacy implies distance,
and Truth is distanceless. You are searching with
the mind, and mind can only search for an object.
Can mind find that in which it itself appears as an
object? If you don't get it, it is okay for the moment.
It doesn't have to make sense. This needs only to be
intuited. You are looking for something, but you are
already looking from that very place. Who gets it?

When there is a 'you' and Truth,
effort has to be made to be one.
When there is you *as* Truth, effort falls away.
What creates this shift?
Not you *and* That, only you *as* That.

349

The greatest *sadhana*
is to abide in the living and effortless
recognition of your own Self.

350

Love is your Self.
It is your real name and the name of every living being.
But you will not truly know and be this self-love
until you are willing to exchange
your identity for Truth.

351

As the personal 'I' disappears
under the piercing light of self-inquiry,
that which witnesses its disappearance
remains as it ever is—pure unmixed joy!

352

Where do you imagine the Truth to be
and behind what can it be hidden?
And from whom?
Think about it.

Just admit:
My life is not in my hands.
It is in God's hands.
Offer yourself up.
Live on God's plate.
Climb into God's soup bowl.
Be willing to be even a single bean
in the Lord's minestrone pot.
Like this, become God's *prasad*.
Don't know how.
Just say Yes and be swallowed up.

Everyone who comes sincerely to satsang
is on death row—the whole lot of them.
They're not on the payroll.
They volunteer to die to the unreal.
If you truly come to satsang,
you must come with this knowing inside.

I wish to meet you.
But I don't want to meet the 'therapy-person'.
Apart from the therapy-person, the one with a complex,
does anybody here have anything left to meet?
I don't even want to talk about 'meeting' actually,
because to meet is not the ultimate.
Meeting is already late.
Something is there before meeting.
I want to meet the one before the concept of meeting.
How? You have to drop everything,
including the notion of 'I' which gives you the sense
and pride of individual autonomy.
Like this, you empty yourself completely.
Don't avoid this opportunity.
Do it now and speak from what remains.
This must be discovered today.
Now, how long will your inquiry go on for?

In the beginning, thoughts appear to veil the Self, but it's not a truth. When you're established in the Self, thoughts can be there. They just don't veil the Self. They cannot replace the Self. And the popular myth that they overshadow the Self is only delusion. Everything arises within the Self. If you think you are a person, you isolate yourself from the whole and suffer. But once you realise you are the Self, all is a harmony.

357

You're waiting for a miracle
to encourage you to enter your Heart.
You plead, 'Prove to me that I will be okay,
and then I will surely let go.'
No.
Let go.

Remain empty.
Resist the pull to go into any state
—your Self is not a state,
or you may say it is a stateless state.
Notice that in simply being here,
there is no need to control the senses or any activity.
You are naturally aware but uninvolved.
Here, the sense of being a person is only a sense.
In looking for the 'person'
you discover it is only an idea.
There is a natural sense of presence.
There is no need to imagine or to create, simply you are.
You are not trying to be—you are.
Do not add any descriptions to the sense of being,
for it is already complete.
Simply be aware of this.

Sometimes there will be an intensification
of your unfolding into the Self.
Be completely open in your heart.
Don't say, 'Okay, I would like to travel in first gear.
It's nice, and I'm coming towards second.'
No. When you surrender,
let God's hand be on the gearstick. Let him drive.
Don't try to control, in any way,
the speed of your deliverance.
Don't suggest slowing down.
Don't say, 'I can only cope with this speed.'
And don't even bother about a seat belt.
Be in full trust.

Apart from thought and imagination,
where else can the sense of separation arise?
There is only the one immutable Self.
Who are you?

Beloved,
while the whole world sleeps
I remain awake in awe of your magnificence.
Though none can attain to you,
none exist apart from or without you.
None but you could reveal such a wonder
inside my heart.

To be in the company of those whose minds and hearts
are turned towards the Truth is to be in the company
of holiness. Don't hold onto any image of what freedom
should be like or how your life will change. Throw
all these things overboard. Just present yourself at
the feet of God with a big Yes inside your heart.

Say, 'Yes. I'm helpless without you. Rid me of ego
and merge me in you. I'm here only for this. I don't
know any way or path. You are my refuge.'

Come to the shrine like this—empty.

The concept 'I' has the capacity
to be either the most holy
or the most profane concept
in the human kingdom.
Find out what discerns this.

Why do you cling to memories so much? Is it because
we have the sense that the present is incomplete? Why
go to past or future? Or even present! Is there not
something even more alive than the present? Pure
presence. As you come to verify this, spontaneously
you will also know that you are the timeless One.

365

When the dark cloud of ego fades away,
that which is unveiled gives light to the world.

366

Don't waste time watching and reacting
to the mind of 'others'.
Your own mind causes more trouble
than the minds of everyone put together.

367

All of God's gifts are great.
Even if God gives you poverty.
There is a wealth in poverty and a poverty in wealth.
Contemplate. Discern. Confirm.

368

The universe is playing on your behalf.
Every move is tailor-made for you.
Even slipping on a banana skin
—all is for your awakening.

369

You are the Self in a dream journey of
losing yourself and having to find your way
back home. Auspiciousness is when the
very dream itself is telling you, 'Wake up.'

We sometimes embody so much worry and fear about
life which is not true of life. You say, 'Life is difficult!' Life
is not difficult. You are living it difficult, you see.
It is everything and anything, depending upon you.
You are the nucleus of the life you are experiencing.

You are not the drifting mind
—notice this.

Liberation is to be
firmly established in nothing.

You are discovering that even the seeker is a phantom.
This one is already late.
You are already here. You are timeless.
When you realise you are timeless, everything else is late.
Because whatever happens, you are already here.
Something is practising to reach you,
but you are already watching this.

374

Life is only now. It can never be tomorrow.
Tomorrow is only a concept.
One of the worst things is to miss the recognition
of your own good fortune.
You are life itself.

375

The self that you are trying to improve does not exist.

376

What is your Master's highest teaching?
I am my Master's highest teaching.

377

Ego will not immediately vanish
upon the realisation of the Truth,
but it will be more quickly and more easily discerned.
Its power keeps diminishing
in the light of Self-recognition
until it becomes insignificant altogether.

Who do you think you are to serve God?
You can't even make a bloody cup of tea without his help.
Come to think of it, you don't even bloody exist.

379

You always desire to get to something or somewhere.
You are ever on the move
from the moment you took the tablet of birth.
But you are looking for something to fill a space
that cannot be filled by any object.
It can only be filled by the subject.
The subject doesn't even have to fill anything.
The subject is totally complete.
The object does not exist.
The object is the subject and the subject is the
object, but the object cannot be by itself.
The object can only exist with the subject,
but the subject exists by itself.
All objects and subjects are only the one subject.
There are no objects.
Do not object to what I am speaking.
Only the object would object,
I'm sure you understand.

380

Truth cannot only comfort you.
At times, it has to cut through to the bone,
to the very marrow even,
if this is what it takes to set you free.

381

Very often people say to me, 'Mooji, I am so unhappy
but you don't seem to care or even want to know what
is going on.' And actually it is true. I don't want to
know what you think is going on. And I don't believe
you. Nothing is going on. You are happy by nature but
think you are unhappy. Your unhappiness is totally
made up. You are just too lazy to look inside yourself.

382

Your true nature is no distance from you. Just recognise
what is always here, unconditioned and untouched.
From the standpoint of human conditioning,
there seems to be a journey. But from the position
of consciousness, this makes no sense at all. Change
from the position of personhood to that of presence;
otherwise you will miss what I am saying. When
inside your heart you understand yourself to
be consciousness, my words will be very easily
understood and assimilated, and delusions will flee.

383

The illusory identity desires to be free
of its delusions and become the true Self.
But is this not only an idea
appearing in front of the true Self?
Who gets it?

384

My most auspicious advice: Remain empty.
Leave all that personal mind stuff aside.
Stay as the impersonal awareness alone.
This is the highest way and choice.
Accept and follow this advice with all your heart.
You will find it sufficient to win you freedom.

385

As pure awareness you are beyond names
and forms, concepts and descriptions.
Comings and goings are noticed from here,
but there is no fuss, no interest.
This is the natural state.
There is no need to hold onto anything here
because there is no fear and there is no need.
You are not imagining, not creating, simply noticing
—and it takes no energy.
Any intention from the mind need not be followed.
In fact, there is no need to follow anything.
You are complete, content and without waiting.
You are neither going nor coming, neither in nor out.
Still you totally *are*.

386

Mind wants to run—let him.
Mind wants to rest—let him.
He wants to climb a tree—let him climb.
But see: Can he climb without you?
Can he rest without you?
Can he run without your knowing?

387

Don't pick up any big jobs
such as balancing life
or trying to be one with the universe.
Mind loves this.
However, the position's already filled.
You needn't apply.

388

No going back. No going forward.
The Supreme is not found in any direction.
Though many go to the East in search of it,
it is not found in the East.
Many go to the West, but it is not found there either.
North, South, up, down, in or out,
nowhere is it found.
A lover of God smells its fragrance
—joy, peace, silence, wisdom and love.
But this flower no one has found.

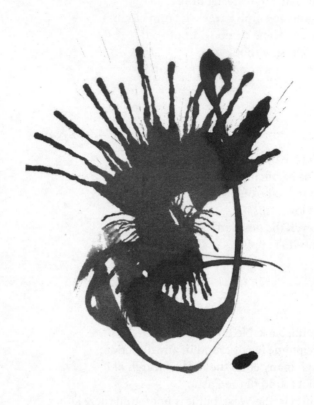

389
You are naturally happy.
Happiness is your true nature.
No one can make you unhappy.
Your imagination alone can do that.

Spontaneous Satsang at Swami Swatantranand Ashram, Rishikesh, India 2014

Spontaneous Satsang at Vasishta's cave, Uttarakhand, India 2013

Mooji at Shree Ma Anandamayi Ashram, Kankhal, Uttarakhand, India 2016

Mooji pays respect to Shree Anandamayi Ma, Kankhal, Uttarakhand, India 2016

Haridwar, Uttarakhand, India 2016

Leaving the Ashram with Swami Swatantranand, Rishikesh, India 2016

Sunset at Monte Sahaja, Portugal 2012

A glimpse of Monte Sahaja, Portugal 2014

Guruji with his daughter, Leah, and the Sangha, Phool Chatti Ashram, India 2013

At home in Monte Sahaja, Portugal 2013

Laxman Jhula, Rishikesh, India 2014

Mooji with young yogis, Rishikesh 2016

Satsang at Papaji Satsang Bhavan, Lucknow, Uttar Pradesh, India 2016

Guruji sharing Satsang at Osho Gangadham Ashram, Rishikesh, India 2014

Spontaneous Satsang by the fire, Monte Sahaja, Portugal 2016

Burn this house down

Sometimes you have the sense that you are coming from the place of the Self—this place has always guided you and you have followed this voice. But it turns out to not be the Self actually. It's your version of the Self. The mind's version. Often this is where other people back off and leave you alone because you say that you're following your God . . . but something is smelly. You are taking a kind of comfort from that space which you think of as your pilot, the space you interpret as what keeps you sane. But you have not been checking-in that sometimes it is the mind itself which imitates the beingness. The ego 'I' can slip behind the seer and say, 'Look, there is only emptiness.' And it's very subtle, but when you catch him, there is such liberation. Then you are truly confirmed in your beingness.

Sometimes we hold back; something wants to defend a certain thing that looks like it is a spiritual truth, but it is just something you are attached to. It can even just be habit. And you have told yourself that this is your guiding light, but it can become an excuse that actually stops you from going beyond. It's like your own bodyguard—but it's not working for the Self. Something is still stopping you from throwing yourself completely in the fire. There is still some holding back.

The ego has many different uniforms. Hesitation is one of its greatest moves—holding back like, 'I've seen this before, done this before. I know what this is all about.' But you have not taken the *darshan* of real seeing yet. This hiding out protects a kind of individuality that seems to safeguard your own unique blend of spirituality. But you have to throw that in. Burn the whole lot down. Burn down this house. Burn it down to DNA, and then put the DNA in the fire also!

390

When you are not you,
then only That is.
And That is you.

391

What great fortune that in this life your heart beats
for Truth. It doesn't matter how much the mind tries to
disturb you. Ignore it. Just remind yourself, 'This life is
for freedom.' No matter how many times mind attacks,
'You're not good enough, not ready. You have not been
chosen.' Don't succumb to this serpent voice. You must
overcome it. Say, 'I am here for freedom and I am free.'
Not that you are choosing to be free, you cannot avoid
being free. God cannot deny the request of the heart.

392

There are no dialogues in the universe.
It is all a monologue
—the one Self conversing with itself
in its favourite concept called 'other'.

393

You are the undying.
Let what is die-able die and let the eternal be.

394

Beloved, I am still floating in the joy of your first kiss.
I am still living in the breath of my first glimpse of you,
O Formless One.

I never stamp anyone's victory as being complete.
It's over when it's over, and not just when your mind
says it's over. Don't give up.
The ego-mind wants you to believe it is over
so it can regain its strength.
Now is your greatest fight.
You must have no compassion towards the unreal.
Strike it with the double-edged sword
of wisdom and devotion to the Real.
This is how you finish him: just stay as awareness.

Don't deprive Grace of her role.
Just say Yes to the true
so that the world may not miss another opportunity
to witness the glory of God unfolding.

The mind is here to test you,
to try and create doubt in you,
to challenge your strength.
You must transcend every doubt about who you are.
Doubts about other things you can afford,
but doubts about yourself,
you must clarify until delusions end.
And mind is very much a part of this dynamic.
As soon as you are clear
you are not the psychological mind
but the immutable awareness,
mind begins to merge with you
as the single Being.

We are both human and divine.

Human troubles compelled the wise
to discover their divine nature.

When you come home to your true heart,
you will become one human being
who stops bothering the world.
Because all are molesting the world
with their thoughts, judgements and projections.
You have stopped.
You have come off the wheel of *samsara*.
You cease to know anything.
Something is switched off
but mystically is still on—beautiful.

In truth, there is not 'us' and 'them'.
Us is them. Them is us. We are That.
All is That. That is all.

When your heart and your mind
are searching for the Truth,
you become instantly beautiful.
You un-become the ugly.
Now you don't need any make-up.
The one who has love for God, or searches for Truth,
is beauty itself. And this company I so love.
We are all here for freedom, but many miss their chance.
All are the children of God,
not step-children, not foster-children, not orphans.
We are ever inside the kingdom of God itself.
And as we meet, even without speaking
and unbeknownst to the mind,
our inner being radiates this light and joy.

402

As a result of one's earnestness for the living Truth,
something begins ripening inside by itself,
becoming sweet and revitalising,
fit only for the mouth of the Beloved.

You, as ego, cannot really care for yourself.
Something has already announced itself:
I am here, inside. Trust.
Now a change has come over you
and you can no longer be the old self.
Just be aware of inner presence
and completely surrender in it.
It is not for the devotee to know
or to assess what is going on.
Do not make any conclusions at all.
There is a sense that something powerful
is present within you.
If you have surrendered yourself,
it is not your business anymore
to take control of your life.
Leave it all to the power and presence.

It is a bit like eating your meal.
You take care that it is cooked well
and that you chew it well,
but once it is swallowed,
it is not in your control anymore.
Now another power is taking care of all that
and it is going to blow you empty.
It is blowing 'you' out.
It is blowing out this deluded personal self
so that you are left with and as
the feeling of timeless Being.
You are being emptied of your story,
of memory, of personhood.
However, there remains a sense of being fully yourself.
Contrary to what many expect or anticipate,
there is a great joy.
What will happen in the future?
This is of concern no more to the one who is liberated.
Time itself is disappearing.
For some beings, it is as though life shrinks down
to a tiny, tiny thing, like an atom,
but inside this atom is the whole universe.
Allow yourself to get quietly absorbed like that.

You say, 'Sometimes when I am in the Absolute,
everything is fine. I even feel to decline sleep, for
the mind may creep back in by morning.'

It all sounds earnest but who is speaking such things?
I know this voice. I know it very well. It is
the voice of personhood. It is the voice of this
world, but it is not real even though it is often
accepted to be the voice of a true seeker.

I cannot say these things everywhere, for my audience
is few. It can seem like there is little compassion
unless I say, 'Don't worry, just keep going, just keep
trying and soon you will reach your ultimate goal.'
But today I am saying, Enough of this! Off with your
head! You, the Self, are already here and complete
inside your own Being, but not as an ego. One needs
only turn away from ego by understanding and
embracing the Truth the Master points out. That is all.

Let's keep it simple, for complexities are almost always
a falsehood in disguise. Only the self-portrait the Self
has of itself as a 'person' can strive for freedom from
the hypnosis of egoic and psychological conditioning,
because this self-portrait functions in duality. The
Self cannot be the outcome of any evolutionary
movement, for it is eternally perfect and whole.

Love is the perfume of Truth.
Truth is the essence of Love.

406

Light is colourless, but when it hits a prism,
a rainbow of colours is expressed.
But they all come from this colourless source.
Similarly, enjoy this colourful life
while knowing it is sourced in your colourless spirit,
without which the rainbow of existence
cannot be perceived.

407

There are no great 'persons'.
Alexander the Great is a myth.
Where is his greatness now?
I don't hear of anyone having a relationship
with Alexander the Great in the heart.
But there was one man
who came riding on a donkey, who,
thousands of years later, no one can forget.
We should really find out what the difference is.

408

However great your knowledge,
if your ego is not removed,
you remain in ignorance.

409

Let yourself be merged into that pure emptiness
which is the presence of God
and true source of all spiritual striving.
Just present yourself genuinely
as a candidate for freedom.
Trust without the need to know anything
such as how well you are 'progressing'
and what is likely to 'happen to you' and so on.
Once the sense of presence awakens within you,
you will have the courage
to surrender everything
to the highest power
and merge your mind inside the Self.

To live with your head at the Master's feet
is to live on top of the world.
This has been my own experience.
Surrender yourself and keep quiet inside your Being.
Don't worry about anything in this world
and your eyes shine bright again.
Your heart becomes open, clear and pure.
Trust.
As you move, Grace goes ahead of you.
Even before you take your first step,
she is there with you and walks with you along the way.
Therefore, lay down your arms.
Lay down all your techniques and your efforts
so that you may discover the effortless silence.
Know that the whole universe
is supporting your awakening.
Neither doubt nor fear. All is well.
Take rest.
Find and feel your Heart again.

411

A wave is ocean, and when it rises up, it is given the
name 'wave'. When it is given this name, it is like it
has an independent existence. It seems to roll along
the surface, which is all water—water flowing in
water—and this we call a life. Then it subsides and
this is called death. Nothing happened to the water. It
is just a spontaneous movement, but because of the
name and the form, it appears as a separate existence.
All the while it is only the play of water rising, flowing,
subsiding—no story. Mind makes the story by
creating an illusory identity. In true understanding,
it is all one. When the identity rises up, we call it
life. When it subsides, we call it death. But really, if
you look from the perspective of the pure Self, there
is no such thing as an autonomous, independent
existence. All actions are the actions of the ocean.

412

All our energies go to our body-mind. There are many
people who at the first sign of a bellyache are ready
to rush to the doctor; they take it that seriously. But
the suffering due to ignorance of the Self is going on
for lifetimes and nobody takes that so seriously.
And this we call life. Isn't it funny?

413

There is no need to transcend
what has no meaning for you.

Everything that happened, you never saw it coming.
The greatest things in your life, you did not expect
—they simply unfolded.
As you begin to recognise and accept this,
you relax and see that your life is unfolding
inside a greater harmony.

Free will, destiny, all of these things
are only pertaining to your body-mind expression,
not to your real Self, which is beyond all that.

Find that which cannot be extinguished
before the candle of this body melts away.

Do not try to hold life to your mind's agenda.
Accept playfully.
Let life be a moment by moment discovering.
Do not strangle life with plans;
let life show you its own mysteries and beauty.
Now your beingness can open,
and your mind and heart will not cultivate fear,
but radiate wisdom, light and joy.

417

You believe in your conditioning
more than you believe in God.
We believe more in our delusions
than we believe in the Truth.
It's like this because we
have a strong belief and attachment to duality,
which is not possible with non-duality.
And we do cling and protect our attachments!
Knowing that non-dual understanding and Truth
is the highest, we can only be That, not become it
—for It alone Is. All else is delusion.

418

Mind says, 'You're still outside but you're almost there.'
It seems very encouraging but as long as you believe
and accept this idea, it will divide you
and send you on a journey of near misses.

419

There will be a moment when you ask the question
'Who am I?' and no answer is found.
No hands go up.
There is just this beautiful silence
and yet nobody is keeping silent.
You cannot be a keeper of silence.
Find and be the silence that has no keeper,
the being that needs no support.
It already shines by itself.

You pierced a hole through the thick veil of delusion
and pulled me through into your holy presence.

Who is there left to say these words, O Wordless One?

421

Don't challenge yourself to be brave or fearless;
challenge yourself to be open
and to trust in the higher Self.
Challenge yourself to remain inwardly still
and centred inside your own being.

422

I don't think I could give you any greater gift
than allowing you to be yourself unapologetically
—to drown completely inside your own ocean.

This is a mighty existence.
If even a fool stops for a moment to reflect
on the great magnificence,
goosebumps will come to shiver at the might of this
universe and sing hallelujah to the Truth.
If they are doing this, why are you holding back?

423

Does the sun know night?
Does it even know day?
You can worship the sun.
You can dry your clothes in the sun,
but this is not the sun's job.
It only shines.
The Self is like this.

424

When the mind comes up, don't say,
'Oh no, the mind came back!'
Who would be saying this?
Don't just take it for granted, find out.
Mind arising should not raise any alarms.
It is merely a phenomenon.
Who is suffering from the mind? Actually, no one.
These are thoughts which, when believed in,
create the illusion that they are real.

Look: isn't there an awareness
of what is referred to as the mind,
including the one who is suffering it?
And is awareness itself suffering?
Can awareness suffer?
You must contemplate this over and over again
until all delusions are dispelled.
This will set you free.

425

Beloved, remember this:
Your life, however it may appear,
is naturally pointed towards awakening to the Real.
Strive for Truth and freedom from the hypnosis
of psychological conditioning.
Do not let the lower tendencies
sabotage your unity with the Supreme
by enticing you with the ephemeral.

426

In the soil of doubt, faith cannot flower,
trust will not grow, spontaneity will not show.
Therefore, avoid the house of doubt.
By all means allow it some space.
It may bring you something also,
like a little time and space to reflect.
But beware of routine doubtfulness, for left unchecked,
it quickly induces fear, suspicion, resistance and identity
—the poorest company one could keep.

427

Shh! Don't talk so much about yourself.
It doesn't even exist, but your talking makes it appear so.
Keep quiet inside your mind and being
and pray that your ego disappears this day.

428

The sage has overcome life
by this very understanding and attitude:
What comes, goes.
What is born, dies.
What is preserved, deteriorates.
Whatever is manifested, returns to emptiness.
I am that emptiness.
I am without name or form.
I am the unchanging and timeless.

429

Use mind sparingly
for it easily flavours life
and overwhelms its real taste.

430

You must come to the stage that when you go out from
here, you remain effortlessly marinating inside your
being all the time. Outwardly, there may be activities,
but internally, you remain the unchanging peace and
serenity. It is only then that weary and tired beings
can take rest in your presence.

If you are easily set on fire and agitated because of the
events around you, you are not sufficiently established
in the Self so that others can take rest in your
presence or recognise themselves in your reflection.

The sage's presence and being is the light of the world.
Of course, all this is not your job, it is simply your joy.

431

What is liberation?
It is to be free of personal identity.
It is to be free from the hypnosis of conditioning;
to be free from the magnetic influence
and compulsiveness of the psychological mind.
It is to recognise that you are not an object,
that this body is an inadequate representation of being,
and is only a vessel through which consciousness and
the vital force act in their portrayal called 'life'.

432

If you have the eyes to look inside
and you are exploring the galaxy of your own being,
you cannot come to the end of what Is.

433

If you want to understand or grasp Truth
in the way that Buddha has,
you will have to disappear personally.
When you disappear personally,
you don't then appear impersonally.
You remain as you are and have always been
—the unchanging and ungraspable Truth.

434

There must either be 'you' living in this body
or God living in this body.
Who does better?
Bear in mind it was God's house in the first place.
Where did 'you' come from?

435

Ignorance is the notion of two.
Knowledge is the notion of one.
Truth is beyond notions.

436

One who has realised the Truth sees that in this play of
duality, beings may appear to love or to hate him. But he
also knows that they cannot really hate him or what he
truly is unless they first hate themselves. He knows that
in reality he is what they are and they are what he is
—the single, indivisible Truth.
Therefore, they also cannot truly hate themselves
unless they are in the state of ignorance of the Truth.

437

All troubles come for and from the personal 'I'.
Let your 'I' be pure consciousness, the Self,
and experience life as joy, peace, love and harmony.

438

It's not what the mind says.
It's how seriously it is taken.

439

There is a great freedom in realising that things don't
have to be perfect in the way your mind would like.
Things are whatever they are—that's not what makes
them fine. What makes them fine is that you are
nothing. Things don't have to be something when you
are nothing. Being nothing is the greatest freedom.

440

Seeker of Truth,
Whatever is born out of time,
you need not be concerned about.
Let life take care of that. Let life take care of life.
Keep quiet and let your mind rest inside your heart.
Don't worry. Right now belongs only to now.
Just be now.
There are no demands, requirements or conditions.
You are simply here. As you confirm this and
pay attention to this simple fact,
the whole world becomes a harmony right in front of you.

441

Though the eyes be open,
let the seeing be empty of identity.

442

Deny yourself. Turn away from the ego's self-interest
and the psychological identity. Keep sweeping it
aside. For a while it may seem that if you reject the
ego, there is nothing else there to experience. Ego, as
personal identity, seems all you know. But this isn't
true, for as you are discarding your old skin, you
are finding your true nature as the Self. And you are
discovering that what you are discarding is a tiny
bubble in the ocean of the real and imperishable Being.

443

You are no thing
presently conceiving of yourself as something.
The body is something,
but without the mind, the body could not be seen.
And without the consciousness,
the mind cannot be seen
And without the Absolute,
the consciousness cannot be seen.
Contemplate this.

444

The Truth can never be missed.
It can only be imagined to be missed.
And at a certain point you will see
Truth is unmissable to itself.

You say you try to slow down the mind enough so
you can stay in the Self, but there is no need to 'slow
down the mind' for this. The mind has never been
able to stay in the Self by effort. This is all due to
much misunderstanding. Please listen: to stay in
something is an effort. It requires a dedication and a
skill. It would require full-time commitment, devotion,
determination, single-mindedness. Even the Buddha
could not do it. People have spent many years naked
in caves trying to convert or merge the mind inside
the heart and have failed. They may have achieved
something they did not have before, like peace or
concentration or even joy, but they retain their identity
as a seeker or practitioner—an entity who attains
something. They may become a peaceful person, but
there is a duality there. They must *be* the peace itself.

The Self cannot be reached or owned by anyone. It can
only be discovered and recognised as the effortless
and natural source of all which Is and appears to be.

How do you ask something as fickle as the mind
to stay in something as absolute as the Self?
Isn't it all a little ridiculous?

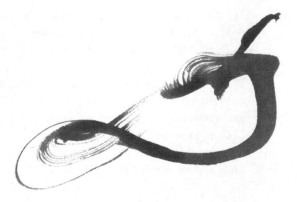

446

Attention pays attention to a lot of things,
but when attention pays attention to attention,
then there is stillness, and in that stillness
nothing is.

447

Sometimes when you are fed up, you just want
the enlightenment pill. But I say, No, no, no.
Maybe if you are free instantly, something could
not cope with it. Something has been preparing
you internally, mentally and emotionally, to cope
with the full impact of seeing. So don't be in a rush
and instead simply walk with me, talk with me and
see if you can follow my words inside your heart.

Fully enjoy the adventure of Self-discovery.

448

For an Advaita *teacher, you seem to express as
both an* Advaitin *and* Bhakta. *It seems a little
confusing, because these paths seem so different.*

Why do they bother about whether Mooji is a true
Advaitin or a *Bhakta*. He has no status. The great masters
and saints are already correctly counted in the house
of God. I am only a lover. Please ignore me. None of
this would have come to light had God not pulled me
aside and whispered sweet Nothing into my ear.

If you want to get the most out of me,
be seated in the position of consciousness
and listen as consciousness itself.
If you listen as a person,
you will never grasp where I am
or what I am pointing to,
because the person has so much conflict inside,
so many differing voices working
to divide, argue and compete.

Listen as consciousness.
Find an attunement, a synchronicity
with the sense of presence.
Be one with it.
This synchronicity is a much higher level
of communication in the realm of being.
It is much higher than conversing
mentally or verbally.
Heart resonance is the vibration of holiness.
Through it, you come spontaneously
to recognise the Self.

450

You cannot imagine, reach or attain awareness.
You can only recognise and be the awareness itself.
And you cannot become awareness
by taking any action.
You can only recognise in the Heart
and acknowledge that awareness is always present.
It is beyond all qualities.
It is unchanging and constant.
It alone truly exists.
It is our source and Self.

451

What is Heaven?
A silent and empty mind.

452

If there were no concepts, would there be 'you'?
Who are you if there are no concepts, no beliefs?
You can find out right now.
Just don't touch any concept,
including the concept 'I' or 'me'.
What does it mean, 'don't touch'?
It means don't combine
or identify yourself with any thought
or object of perception, real or imagined.
Therefore, don't even identify with your person.
Avoiding this, what remains?

453

Real understanding leading to liberation
takes place in presence, not in the person.
Therefore, your initial effort is to lift the consciousness
from the personal state to the state of unmixed presence.
Only when you are synchronised
in presence as presence itself
does Self-discovering become an effortless joy.
Then self-inquiry is not merely something you practise,
it becomes the mirror you look into
to see the face of God.

454

The sky does not have to exist without clouds
to be pure sky.

455

I'm not pointing you to something you have to
remember. In classical knowledge, you have to
remember things. Why do you have to remember
things? Mostly because they don't have a true life
of their own; they are not natural to you. You may
think, 'But I have to remember the Self because
that's the number one thing I've forgotten.'
I'm going to drop a bomb on you about this:
that you have forgotten your Self is *itself* an
idea. You cannot not be the Self. You may
somehow be distracted by another idea you
have, but this is a learned ignorance.

You don't have to fight.
You only have to keep choosing Truth. Only choose.
Let Grace fight for you if needed.
You just keep choosing, 'Yes, I choose the true.'
And when the exposing power comes,
be completely naked in front of it.
This much courage you must have.
When the impulse arises
to look deeply into a thing, be fearless,
because the power is with you in this moment.

Be empty. That's it.
When you're empty, you're the most powerful,
because you're present.
You're awake. You're alive.
And you're nothing.

457

Don't worry about anything at all.
You are not here by accident.
This form is just a costume for a while.
But the one who is behind the costume,
this one is eternal. You must know this.
If you know this and trust this,
you don't have to worry about anything.
This world is so full of love.
And your heart, your being,
is so full of love, so full of peace.
You don't have to go
to some place else to find peace.
It is right where you are.

458

Very few beings on this planet will refer to themselves
as pure consciousness, as emptiness.
Have you heard anyone speaking like this?
You cannot say things like this.
You could get locked up for this,
but even if they lock you up,
they just think they've got you locked up.
You, the pure Self, cannot be locked up at all.
What you find is that the whole world is
inside the jail and you are out!
They themselves are in the prison of egoic identity,
feeling sorry for you being in prison.
but actually, you are the one who is free.
How ironic!

459

It doesn't matter how things feel. Don't use feelings
as a gauge for assessing whether things are right or
not. There is a clarity that is much more profound
than just feeling. Feelings and moods come and go
and are perceived. The tendency to identify with
feelings and thoughts is also perceived. Somehow,
the one who perceives is the most overlooked.
This is what I am pointing to over and over again:
although consciousness perceives the momentary,
it also has the power to ignore everything.
It is ever untouched and unstainable.
You alone can confirm this to be true.

460

The book of your Being is open.
The pages are empty.
Let the Divine write something inside your heart.

461

The Self does not destroy;
it's just that in its presence delusions vanish.

462

You say something is efforting to find Truth.
But that which is observing this, is that also efforting?
Contemplate this deeply
and embrace your freedom.

463

There is a way to again be in real time with the universe,
but it is not through force, imagination or manipulation.
It is by finding your true Self.
When you do, you will not need to manipulate life,
it will simply flow.

464

Through the power and grace of the Master,
the identity and personality that you feel is yours
is becoming more light, ephemeral.
One day you will ask, 'Who am I?'
but instead of an answer,
an old perspective, disguised as a person,
will no longer be found.
In that moment you will be established
in your true nature.

465

Satsang is to make you empty again.
Only in emptiness are you relieved of your suffering.
Only from here is your seeing panoramic.
And it is not a practice.
All that has to happen is that I strip you of all concepts.
Then you don't have to be convinced by me
that you are emptiness.
You will be convinced naturally. Spontaneously.
It is just the outcome of true seeing.

466

There is no conflict in you, the Self.
If there is conflict, it is between thought and thought.
As long as the sense of 'I' and 'other' is believed
in, conflict is inevitable.
Through self-inquiry, confirm again and again:
I am the Self, the complete and indivisible whole.

467

Let the mind buzz. Just recognise what is not buzzing.
There is a stillness here that no movement can touch.
It is our real home which has been deserted by us
while we are infatuated with the world of mirages.
Though deserted, it is not a desert.
It is the divine oasis, the source from which all springs.

216

468

I say sometimes that 'I'
is the slimmest letter in the alphabet,
and yet the whole world is hiding behind it.
You cannot hide behind Yes,
because Yes is so innocent, so pure.
The mind wants some elaborate techniques,
but in the end, the heart's Yes is enough.
Say, 'Yes, I am here for this, rid me of ego
and merge me in you,' or some beings say,
'Replace me with you,
remove what is not true here,
let me be true forever.'
And so your whole life
can be a life of Yes to the true.
Truth never takes sides. It has no favourites.
It embraces the whole world as its child.
And that is every living being.
Love is our deepest connection.
When we turn to love, not merely agreements,
we come alive again to what is real
and to what brings lasting happiness in this world.

469

You never hear a prophet or a sage say, 'I think,'
or, 'This is my opinion.' Why? Because they have lost interest in
the personal sense of self. For them, it really doesn't exist and has
no credibility at all. The liberated being, free of egoic identity and
its influence, becomes the embodiment of the universal Self.

470

Who in the world allows you to be empty? Emptiness
carries such a stigma. To be empty of the idea of what
you want to do in the future can seem frightening.
But has anybody ever tasted the future? We have so
many ideas like, 'You should at least have a picture,
have a notion, have a dream to pursue.' No one
questions these things. Why are you so obsessed
with the future? You don't even know where you
are now! And you certainly don't question who you
are. If you don't know who you are now, how are you
going to know how you're going to be in the future?

471

If you experience that the source,
which is your real Self,
cannot be perceived phenomenally,
that it is not an object
—not even the most beautiful object
or anything produced from imagination—
then you have solved this powerful mystery
and are free forever.

472

Enter fully your own inner ocean of Being.
You keep coming up to breathe the stale air of the mind.
Therefore, I keep holding your head under the
waters of the Self so that you may drown.
Fear not. You will not drown into death
—you will drown into eternal life.

473

Throw yourself inside now.
Take nothing with you.
You will find me there.

474

Realising that we are the beingness,
that pure and imageless awareness,
knowing this with your entire Being
and being able to let the life force
and consciousness unfold its play
in the presence of that seeing,
you will intuitively know
that you cannot come to an end
of what you are.

475

Due to the light of your own satsang,
mind may be bringing every demon from hell
to stop you from going through the gate to Nirvana.
Don't worry.
Everyone who has found freedom experienced this.
God is with you.
There is a passage in the Bible.
In the psalms of David it says,
'Even though I walk through the valley of the shadow
of death, I will fear no evil for you are with me;
your rod and your staff, they comfort me.'
Your attitude should be to offer everything up
to the heart of life,
to God—your inmost Self.
Hold firm in your resolve for Truth.
Your spirit is mighty in the Lord
and will transcend everything.

476

Life does not make decisions.
The universe is not planning itself. It just unfolds.
Look at this plant. It is without concern.
It doesn't say, 'I think maybe in a few days
I will put a new leaf just here to my left.'
The plant is not thinking.
Its life is a spontaneous unfolding.
Like this plant, our lives can unfold
in effortless grace and joy.

477

I come to you and challenge you.
What is so precious in your life and about you
that is worth exchanging eternity for?
What are you holding onto so tightly
that is more valuable than timelessness?
What are you keeping in this life
when even this body you cannot keep?
What is so precious to you in this life of yours
that you keep Truth suspended, paused,
and you can't separate
from your attachments or your fear?
You don't trust that life can take care of you better
than you can take care of yourself.
Why is it that we are so loyal to identity
and its projections and delusions?

478

I am totally in love with nothing.

You say that you can see
everything is coming and going,
but that you yourself are not coming and going.
You say you have glimpses of the Truth,
but then you say fear arises, a fear of death.
Something inside says, 'One more step and you will
never be able to come back. It will be irreversible.'
But I want to ask you something:
can it be the pure Self that is saying this?
If not, then who is speaking?
Now you are right at the door of Nirvana
and something wants to run away,
because there is a fear that all will be lost.
But what do you have to lose?
The ego is playing its biggest card yet
—the ace up the sleeve of the mind itself.
Everybody has at least one biting concept
that keeps them behind the line of the mind.
'It's irreversible!' says the mind,
'You won't be able to come back.'
Back to what?
Reflect.
Who understands that all of this is a powerful illusion?

Presently you think you are mixed up with the
mind and are trying to disentangle yourself from
the turmoil of thoughts. But both the mind and
the one trying to disentangle from it are unreal.
This is perceived in the Real.

481

Let life unfold without identity.
Leave space for the unexpected.
Give up the habit of predicting,
interpreting and projecting.
Simply stay in the neutrality of Being
so that you perceive all from the Heart-mind.

482

Without knowing oneself as what one truly is,
all else is speculation.

483

The one medicine for everything is to know your
Self. You have to awaken to your true position as
the formless witness of all that appears. When
this recognition occurs, a great sickness is over, a
great burden is set free, a joy is released and there
arises within the heart tremendous gratitude to
existence, to the Self, to God who is Truth.

484

The mind is like an inner journalist that attacks
your self-image and then reports about it. But
all the time there is a higher seeing within
that is not caught in the bubble of this play.
This seeing is you.

You say you don't know how to make this magic
that I am talking about happen.
Well, 'you' cannot make it happen.
The magic is there when 'you',
the 'person', are not there!
What am I referring to as 'you'?
The psychological identity or ghost
who suffers from its own projections
—the imagined self.
When this one is no more,
everything becomes magical.

You have to go beyond this person
you imagine yourself to be.
Truly speaking, no one is interested
or can be interested in you, the person,
for the person is a selfish and limited form
of consciousness.
I am also not interested in anyone,
only in their true being.
The least interesting or engaging thing
in meeting anyone is their story,
for the person, along with their story or self-image,
is a construct, a pretence, a rumour, a myth.
You are the Infinite,
and I am not paying you a compliment by saying this.
I am only saying out loud
what you know deep inside your being,
but have seemingly forgotten.

487

Your life used to belong to you
—at least you had this feeling.
But now it is belonging to God,
and you are slowly melting and merging here.
At a certain point you will disappear.
When you disappear, unexpectedly you will find
you are fully here in the most alive way.
This is the mystery, a paradox
that the mind will not easily accept.
It will fight against anything that threatens its existence.
Trust is the key. Stay open.
Live with a Yes inside your Heart for all that is true.

488

When mind-storm strikes—cut or unplug.
Avoid engaging in any story or analysis.
Instead, immediately cut the juice of attention
and unplug from the mind current.
This is the marvelousness of impersonal witnessing:
that simply by keeping one's attention in the state of
neutrality, mind returns to its natural abode
as unborn awareness.

489

To awaken to the Truth is not an event.
In the falling away of delusions,
a recognition of the ever present,
unborn and immutable Self
is revealed in immense joy.

490

You are beauty itself.
Beauty is not merely a physical thing.
It is a heart that is open to God,
to Truth, to existence itself, fearlessly.

491

The awakening of the Self does not always happen
in one whack. It is meant to be like that. There is a
gradual merging of the ego-mind with the Heart-
mind through the yoga of perfect knowledge, and
this expresses as the harmony of being. The mind
has to slowly adjust to the atmosphere of the Self.

492

Mind has a very important role in the play of life.
It is a wonderful power that emerges from the same
source as the conscious being we are. However, as soon
as you believe yourself to be only a person, mind is
going to bite you, and it is good that it bites, because
this bite tells you, 'Each time you turn to me in need,
I am going to bite you until you leave me alone and
stand on the firm ground of your own Truth.'

493

It's not important where the urge for freedom comes
from. The important thing is that it is here. It is the light
that guides one back to freedom itself. It will serve to
dispel all delusions and thus set your heart free.

494

Let the untrue be exposed and thoroughly burned.
Sometimes the way into that completeness,
that recognition, is that whatever is untrue is rejected
as it is recognised as false, either by you or by me.
And you may be thinking, 'Oh my God, I really thought
I was getting somewhere! This is so discouraging...'
And so your world feels like it is turned upside down.

Do not be disheartened.
Instead keep an attitude of gratitude.
It is your good fortune that your 'world' is being crushed. I myself
don't have a world.
Let yours be upside down
so that what is true in you can reveal itself
and begin unfolding in its authentic expression
as true life and being.

Grace is helping you in every way. Trust it.
Say, 'Yes, I am here, remove this sense of separation,
this arrogance of separateness and merge me in you,
O God, O Universal Being, Self, Truth, Life.
Don't give me any technique. Absorb me.
Replace me with You.'
And finally: trust your Master.

495

There is an innocence here, a purity that does not
even know that it needs to search for anything, but
paradoxically, it causes all this search to come into play.

496

Just quietly vanish inside yourself. Disappear.
So beautiful.
Your form is still here, but inside, nobody. Inside, cooked.
But don't tell anybody that.
Just be the peace of this world,
the light and joy that shines from the indivisible Self.

497

The one who prays to God
should not pray regarding God as 'other'
but as the core, the all-encompassing essence of Truth.
Then this one and what he seeks is satisfied
in the realisation that life is lived
as answered prayers.

498

Don't be concerned with your own growth,
with how much progress you are making.
Forget about it.
Give up this notion that you must know or
understand so many things before you will be free.
Just keep falling in love with the Self.
Be fully consumed by love.
Love blossoms into knowledge,
and together, they set you free.

499

You seem to have unending questions, and doubt after doubt fills your mind. This is due to an argumentative mind. You must observe this tendency until it is clear your real Self is apart from this. Believe and trust in the Master's simple and clear guidance. Follow it as though your life and sanity depends on it. Like this, doubt, arrogance and all resistance will fade away.

500

Know that the sense of finding and losing the Self is illusion. Know also that the advice to 'stay as the Self' is also illusion. Know that there is no one to find the Self, for the Self alone is. The Self alone creates all this game in order to taste the experience or the play of separation and union. There is only ever the one indivisible Self.

501

Being in satsang, you as ego are being scooped out from inside and replaced with emptiness.
But it is not a dead emptiness.
It is the spirit of God.

That which is effortless alone is natural.
It is not trying to be or become anything.
It simply is.
Is there a recognition of this or not?
It is constant.
In fact, it does not even know constant.
It knows nothing at all.
But there is a sense of knowing arising in
That which cannot be known.
It is referred to as the ultimate knower,
yet it cannot be known nor does it know anything.
To the ignorant,
the things of heaven sound strange,
like hocus-pocus.

God knows nothing. Why?
Because there is nothing independent of God.
There is nothing apart from Truth to know.
You must hear and feel my words not merely
as words but as spirit and truth.
Therefore listen with full attention
and inside your Heart,
because this is not merely a mental exercise.
Actually the mind gets exorcised by the Master's words.
The Buddha's words are direct, timeless, immediate.
My words must resonate.
In the search for Truth,
resonance is the fastest and highest way.
Through synchronicity, everything is assimilated
very easily like a natural osmosis.
Just you are.
This knowledge is the goal of all earnest striving.
'I am'—there is nothing apart to report.
You just quietly drown inside your own ocean
and what emerges out of that absorption
is a book the world has not yet read.
The book is writing itself in its very unfolding.
The author and the book are One.

503

Sometimes you look into the face of a human being
and only being is seen. No history is left there.
You are looking into the face of God.
The breath of God burns all sorrow and suffering,
all dreams, desires and time,
revealing God's unmasked face.
I love that face.
Now you are looking into the face of God himself.
He is looking into his own face.
If duality has a real purpose,
it is that God may look at God
and enjoy his perfect reflection.

504

Can you come to the edge of yourself
beyond which you are not?

505

When you're looking from the person, you are a person.
When you're looking at the person, you are presence.
When you search sincerely for what the person is,
the whole thing is revealed as just an idea.

506

You are here before the sense 'I am' arises.
What could you possibly be?
Ponder, don't speculate.
Stay open. Stay fresh.
Leave some room for surprise.

What truly is is timelessly here but it cannot be seen
because the one looking for it expects
to find it as an object.
This seeking one is itself an object
appearing in the expanse of the subject.
The object has no independent reality.
You've only been used to looking
from the perspective of a person,
so it is not yet clear that you are
the pure untouched presence.
You are not an object.
You are the subject.
Understand this:
you cannot see the subject.
You can only *be* the subject.
Objects are only your dreaming.
All is the subject alone!

The manifestations of consciousness are unending.
Nothing in the universe is fixed.
But my encouragement is not to get too involved with any
phenomena. Let them flow, and remain in and as
the space of inner neutrality. Be empty.
Like this, the personal mind will be quickly
absorbed into the Absolute.
Don't be afraid.
The Real is not some abstraction, some black hole.
It is your complete Self and the most true.
It is always here.
Your aspiration for eternal life comes from here.
Don't be afraid of that.

509

You don't 'have' a life, you are life itself,
and simultaneously, the witnessing of life
in all its varied expressions is perceived in you.

Reflect: if life is what you have then you will lose it one
day, for all possessions are impermanent. Such a belief
automatically places us in the position of the body-mind
and person, which are time-bound and perishable.

But when we come to the understanding that we are
life itself, then all fears dissipate as this understanding
places us in the position of consciousness, which
is formless, timeless and imperishable.

The belief that we are merely our bodies makes us
anxious and hurried, for on a subconscious level
we are driven to get as much as we can before it
all ends. This has been the ongoing trauma of the
human being throughout the ages. However, as
consciousness itself, we are not time-bound. As we
come more into the knowing of this, our minds
and world become wiser and more peaceful, for we
know inside our hearts that we are the timeless.

510

Your love for the Ultimate
must draw you in completely.
It is not a relationship that can last.
It is a very short-term relationship.
It is a one-night stand, actually.
And there will be only One left standing
—the indivisible Self.

511

Where is silence until you discover it?
Where is peace until you find it?
Where is the real Self while you are searching for it?
And who might you be?

512

If you are merely collecting concepts,
you quickly become full of noise.
Only out of emptiness
can spontaneity dance so beautifully.
When a thing needs to be known,
it comes spontaneously out of that immensity.
When it has satisfied its expression,
it goes again back into emptiness unforced.
No report. No burden. No comment.

513

The one in whom the sense of
'I' and 'other' prevails, suffers.
When this duality ends,
undisturbed peace prevails.

514

As soon as one enters the arena of authentic
Self-discovery, the psychological mind starts
to throw up distractions in order to put you
off your goal, and so a battle begins internally.
There's no reason why you should lose this battle.
In fact, you cannot lose, because the enemy
itself depends on you for its life. Know this.

515

The fall from grace
is to somehow contaminate the 'I am'
with the belief that it is a person.

516

You are God's present being unwrapped.
Don't identify with the paper.

517

You know you exist.
This is so natural not even your parents
had to teach you that.
You instinctively know you are alive
and that you are perceiving somehow.
Not even deliberately, it is just happening.
It is an effortless functioning.
And there is awareness of that functioning.
What more can be said?
The rest is entirely made up.

518

This language I'm speaking, your heart alone
knows. Your mind does not know it. This language
I'm speaking is not English or French or anything
else. Your heart alone knows what I am speaking. It
understands without study. Mind is the realm of
time, effort and concepts—the most limited field.

I Am. Without effort, I Am—boundless, limitless, free.

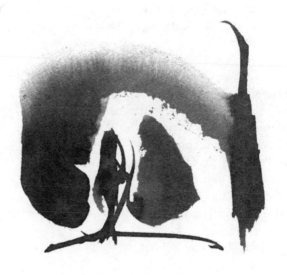

519

You close your eyes and see darkness,
but it is by the light of consciousness
that darkness is seen.

I can never be tired of you.
I can only be tired of your notion of being a person.
Sometimes I get impatient with you:
Why are you still wallowing in this mess?
Come out of this.

As soon as you come out,
all rubbish begins falling away fast.
First you go uphill with your ego,
and then you start going downhill
and everything is coming out.
First, building up, building up, more and
more stuff...getting stuffed, constipated
with concepts...and then? Big bang.
Big laxative, full diarrhoea.
This is freedom.
Every thought is coming out.
You are so happy, so light.
You don't know what to do with yourself.
You are weightless now, completely empty.
Now let it be your quiet understanding
and live fully from this place of joy.

521

The inherent wisdom is within.
With the urge for Truth you will discover it.
It will destroy all delusion.
But in order for it to blossom and bloom,
you must place your head at the feet of God,
or dissolve your identity in unmixed consciousness.
Your heart has to become wide and open,
and filled with devotion, surrender
and the urge for freedom.
Then that mighty power will arise.
It does not destroy;
just in its presence all delusions disappear.

522

The only cause of trouble in the world
is you posing as a 'person'.
How can something as obvious as this
be missed or even grasped?

523

Father Lord,
Thank you for the power of discernment,
experience of life,
for the joy of being,
for the field of harmony, grace,
and this deep contentment inside my heart.
And beyond all this,
thank you for the knowledge
and unbroken experience
of unity with you
as the immutable Oneness.

At a certain point, somebody may call your name and
the response to that call seems to evoke the memory
of 'a somebody' but then attention goes scanning and
finds that this 'somebody' cannot be found.
What did the caller intend to engage?
Who was being called?
Nobody can be found and yet response occurs.
It is the same one who has been responding
through every name but it is not the name.
The real quest is to discover this for yourself.
The seeker is quietly disappearing
in the joy of the discovery.
Don't be in a hurry to share this.
Just keep dissolving.
Everything you do from now on
will carry the fragrance of the Supreme
and evoke in the minds of others
a remembrance of That.
One's very presence becomes a trigger
for the remembrance of God
even though one does nothing at all.

525

Often, in the very moment
the flower of pure consciousness is opening,
some fear, nervousness and agitation comes up,
or a sense of being lost.
But something discerns
that this is not the old kind of lost feeling.
It is not the same old confusion.
There is something exciting about this confusion;
it is like you are on the cliff of the universe.
Sometimes you have to be on the edge
of the seat of your own life,
not always hiding under the bed looking out.
You have to be willing to stand on the cliff
of your own existence
and feel the air of infinite possibilities
that you have never dared to breathe before.
In such a moment you will not know a millisecond
of what is in front of you.
Nor will you be overly concerned.
Facing the great abyss, you will say, 'Here I am, take me.'
And then plunge into the ocean of your own Source.

526

When you look into the eyes of the Beloved,
you become absorbed into emptiness itself.
You lose your duality and become one
beyond even the concept of oneness.
Today, you must find the truth
of your own Self and be that,
for unless you know yourself,
you will not know what true love is.
Love and Truth are one.

527

If God is infinite then surely God must also be in you.
Can it be infinite everywhere else except you?

528

You cannot speak about this.
You cannot show it,
and yet when you come to this place inside your
heart, you will know, 'I am nothing but this,'
and many will somehow recognise you.
They will see you, they will feel your presence.
You don't have to speak anything,
because it is not your words.
Out of the pores in your body
the evidence of Truth will shine.
You are Here, you are Here, you are Here.

Sahaja Moments, Portugal

Editing White Fire, Little Jamaica 2014

View of The Ruins 2013

Christmas Day Satsang in The Ruins 2013

With Krishnabai 2014

Guru Purnima in the Sri Mooji Mandir 2014

Building of the Shiva Temple,
Monte Sahaja, Portugal 2014

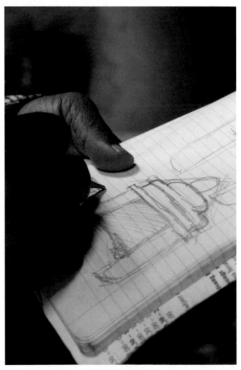

First sketches of the Temple's inner shrine

Baptised in the Heart

Sometimes I meet beings who say they have realised the Self. They believe or claim that they know and understand the Truth. They say they sense it, feel it and are convinced it is what they are and so on. However, it is often sensed here that the mind takes credit for this understanding and purchases further life as the egoic 'achiever' of ultimate Truth. Consequently, the realisation does not get baptised in the Heart and a real chance of freedom gradually fades away.

Such beings can retain their sense of personhood unknowingly. Some even edit my words to fit in with their personal inclinations, projections and spiritual fantasies, but I want to burn all of this to the ground so that they attain true freedom.

What we speak about here is authentic transcendence. One has to overcome the hypnosis of personal conditioning. They have to be free from the psychological influence of the mind. I don't mean that you should 'stop' your mind but rather focus on the witness of mind. It has to be an authentic transcendence, not a Hollywood awakening.

Sometimes I say I don't want or feel for your company. You indulge too much mental and psychological noise. There are too many relationships going on inside your mind. Your representations of yourself physically, mentally, emotionally and psychically are not authentic expressions of the Self. Such a localised identity is not enough at this level of understanding, insight or, we could say, Self-knowledge.

To the ignorant, the sense 'I am' means 'I am the body.'
To the saint, 'I am' means 'I am presence.'
To the sage, 'I am' is the Absolute.

Some beings come to see
that the sense of presence is also perceived.
When you are in the position whereby
even the sense of presence,
the 'I am' itself, is perceived,
then you are in the unnamable,
the unchanging, the ever pure.
And yet you haven't moved
for this understanding to reveal itself.

The vastness that is seen by the mind is not the Self.
The vastness in which the mind is seen is the Self.

532

From the highest perspective,
you're never going to be something.
Get over it!

533

As long as the person is watching, the show goes on.
But if the so-called watcher is itself watched,
then it is clearly also an object.
The ego-sense also has the capacity to observe,
but it observes with self-interest.
As soon as this is grasped,
a greater space opens up within
whereby this watching identity is proven to be unreal.
What remains that sees all this? Find out.
For a genuine seeker,
this is an end-of-the-road question.

534

The life that is known cannot be what I am.
That which cannot be known—That I am!

535

Who is the mind actually speaking to?
You assume it is to you, the Self,
but it is only to your self-image,
the ego which you imagine is your true self.
But are you ready and willing to look at this?
There is a reluctance to question our assumptions,
because it feels like gambling with everything
you believe you have and are.
We want to feel OK, but not K.O.
You want to feel 'okay' with your projections
rather than having them 'knocked out' cold.
Stop protecting that which is suffocating
your true freedom.

536

Why record the act and object of perception and miss
the perceiver? That which gives birth to thousands
of playmates but itself no one can find. Be That.

537

It is said we came here to taste delusion
and then to transcend it.
It is as though consciousness, which is pure in nature,
created a game of seeming imperfection
in order to have the experience of transcending it all.
All this life is a play of transience.
Everything is impermanent, yet divine.
But what you are is timeless.
Each one is a manifestation of the presence of God
wearing the garment of time.

538

Nothing to create, nothing to destroy.
The breath is moving, blood flowing,
body resting, senses open, unforced.
Harmony prevails everywhere.
Listen to the sound of the wind,
delve inside your own stillness and silence.
Nothing needs to change.
It is as it is. All one.
Look at this silence within, this stillness you are
—it lacks nothing, needs nothing,
opposes nothing, claims nothing.
At one with all that is.

539

Beloved Father,
You alone are. This alone is to be remembered
in this body for which purpose it was made.

540

Your body can continue expressing in a natural way.
Intelligence is there. Emotions can come.
Everything can play,
but inside there is total serenity and peace.
No planning, no strategising,
no personal identity is there.
Just the space of pure being.
It is what we are, but we dream and believe we are not.

541

Death can only be terrible if you were only the body.
But you are the imperishable Self.
This life is only for discovering and confirming
this inside your Heart. Amen.

542

People ask me, 'How did you wake up?
How did you do it?'
I say, I didn't do it, it did me.
Actually, it undid 'me'.
And the same one that undid me
is now inside this body trying to undo 'you'.

543

Even when there is nothing happening,
there is the witnessing of nothing happening.

544

When you don't know yourself,
you think others can know you,
but when you know what you are,
you realise no one can know you.
No one can grasp the magnificence
of that which you are.

545

It is far more important
to keep the mind silent and empty
than to attempt to work out
its complexities and idiosyncrasies.

546

Just remember, when you are called by Truth,
it is a calling that comes from the universe.
Satsang is the changing room in which you,
the Buddha itself, are slowly undressing from
all your tight and heavy conceptual garments
into the nakedness of Being.

547

You never lose what you give,
you only lose what you try to keep.

548

The ghost is imagining what it is like to be real,
what it is like to be alive,
but this ghost is itself watched
from the life you are.

549

You should not allow yourself to be conquered by fear,
especially fear born out of insecurity to do with your life.
How many lives you've had, I don't know.
How many situations you've had, I don't know.
Where are they now? They're behind you.
I don't even know if they're behind you.
They don't exist!
And your knees are rattling in this present one
which will soon be past and forgotten.
Take the courage to say, 'I won't live like this.'
Call the bluff of the mind
and tell him to throw his best punch.

550

All the life stories you speak of
are the product of memory and imagination.
Can memory remember itself?
Who makes use of memory?
Is this one the product of memory?
Is this one remembered?
To whom am I speaking?

551

You are the one complete Self
beyond even the concept of completeness.
This is not merely a feel-good experience;
in fact, good or bad, right or wrong,
these ideas and concepts are far away from you here.
Recognise yourself without any definition,
without any description, without goal,
without past, without future,
without desire, without need.
There are no stories here, and yet you fully are.
Here, mind has no power,
because you are not in a state of distraction.
Be aware even of the subtle sensation of presence
as it expresses inside this body.
You are here, yet at the same time
you are beyond every description,
every concept, every feeling
—being the perceiver of them.

552

Avoid cynicism, arrogance and judgement of others
and life, for this more than any other evil blinds you to
seeing the glory and miracles of God in your daily life.

(Sometimes God reveals himself in the very
thing or one you have been judging and you
find yourself bowing at the feet of that one.)

553

If you can, prove to me that you can stand
one step outside of wholeness.
Take one step outside into 'outside of wholeness'.
Can you do it? Because wholeness must include you.
You are at the nucleus of the wholeness.
Your Self means wholeness.
Actually your Self means holiness.

554

The wise do not need to choose their teachers.
They gain or learn from everyone,
from both the foolish and the wise.
Even from the arrogant they learn something.
Therefore their mind retains its universality.
Be inspired by them.

555

Father,
Who else but you has placed the sense 'I am'
inside this body and dwells here?
Who else could be involved?
You, who alone exist, have fashioned this clever idea
called 'me' to experience the feeling of being separated
from you and to seek your grace to find the Truth,
which is no other than yourself.
But now the game is up!
I have found you, who are myself only.
Now where can you hide? How mischievous you are!

556
You don't have to always transcend.
You can also just be nothing.

557

You spend all your money to travel across the world
in search of a spiritual master...and you finally meet
one. Then, out of nowhere, another one shows up.
You think, 'Look! Two masters! How lucky can I be!'

All this is the falsehood of the ego that is forever on
the run. The ego is a mask we make up and wear
while we are not yet ready to simply be our Self. It
is really afraid of meeting the true Master, who is
only the perfect reflection of our real being. Now
fear comes because such an encounter signals the
end of the delusion we have invested energy in for
so long. So you allow your mind to cook up some
excuse and pretend it is double auspiciousness.

I want to tell you something: this kind of farce has
been going on for thousands of years and perhaps
thousands of lifetimes. You may not be aware
of this until a master points it out. Perhaps this
is why we are still drifting about on this planet
playing the game of spirituality. Wake up!

558

If in your heart you have chosen Truth,
then trust your experience
because something guides and protects you.
When your search is genuine
and your heart is humble,
life protects you.
But if you keep some arrogance,
be sure trouble will come.

You say you have been having a series of *satoris*, but
right now it seems like nothing is happening and you
worry that something is missing. Listen carefully now,
what I'm saying is very important: Don't search for
any experiences, even beautiful experiences. Instead,
just be and allow yourself to see what is not an event.

Don't miss this. It is more valuable than any *satori* . . . if
by *satori* you mean an experience that can pass. What
I am pointing to is always present, but everybody has
been missing it by searching for the next experience.
This is only a habit of the mind. And I am not even
pointing you to go to it, but rather calling you to
recognise this timeless reality within yourself.

You are not going to enter into an unconscious state,
but a stateless state. It is the most exquisite state.
I don't even want to call it a state,
because all states come and go in its presence.
However, the Self does not come or go.
It simply Is. Seek confirmation within yourself.

You cannot know what love is.
Just be love. How to be love?
You cannot do it. No one can do it.
It is already timelessly present
here inside as your inmost being.
It is all that you are and more than you can know.
Love is God.

561

From the light of one candle,
a million candles can be lit
without affecting the original flame.
From the single awareness,
innumerable flames of apparent separate existences
are lit and are burning with the same fire.

562

Only when one becomes exhausted of the person
does it become possible to emerge as the Being.

563

Put selfless truth and loving devotion first,
then wisdom will shine forth.
When wisdom accompanies love,
Truth becomes self-evident
and showers countless blessings upon the world.

564

The one the Master guides is the one the Master kills.
But what an auspicious death:
the vanishing of the unreal.

565

There is a peace that does not go.
It does not want to go and it does not want to stay.
It has no place to go. It is.
It has no appointments to be somewhere else.
Allow yourself to fall away from the shape of your mind.
And don't ask how.

566

When you only half suffer you can hold it,
but if you fully suffer you will drop it.

567

You say you want to get rid of the noise,
but you and the noise go together.
You have to be you without 'you' and all noise will stop.
The real you is the formless witness within.
The person, the noisy one, is only imagined.

568

From the place where nothing happens,
you may enter a place where something seems
to happen and enjoy all the seemings of happenings
while knowing nothing actually really happens.

569

When you choose life, life chooses you;
when you choose freedom, freedom chooses you.
The moment your heart turns towards itself,
your mind turns towards Truth.
There is nothing that you are going to find in life
that can compare or compete with a liberated mind.
This is your natural being, your good fortune.

570

Throw out your notions and don't know anything at all.
Don't know anything at all! Why bind yourself?
Let the universe take care of your needs
but do not be needy.
This is a message for the mature.

571

Go through this forest called existence
and come out the other side as Buddha,
as the pure Christ Light,
as Shiva Being.
This forest can take lifetimes . . .
and yet this forest is a dream.

I am open to meet you, all of you. When I look at you,
I can sense energetically whether you are involved in
thought or not. Sometimes I say you have thinking
eyes. I want to meet you beyond mind, more pure than
the thinking eyes. I want to meet *you*. 'About you' I
have heard, but the actual you I have not as yet met.

Is it possible to meet the one of whom I speak?
Take off your costume 'I'-dentity so that you
remain without you, so you are unveiled of you.
Do you follow?

Nowhere in the world are you asked for a meeting like
this. No one is prepared for it. Not even your parents.
Not in any social circles you may go to, not in the pub
nor in the gym, not in the temple, synagogue or church
will you find anyone who wants a real meeting with you
in the way that I mean. They don't even want to meet
themselves as yet. The priest does not want to meet
you. He is far too busy. But here in satsang, everything
is prepared for such an encounter. I want to meet
You. Today, this moment, is as good as any moment.
And I am ready. Is this possible? Can we look at each
other without eyes of differences or 'otherness'?

The only way we can meet like this is once you come
to know yourself non-dualistically—beyond quality,
beyond time, conceptual projections or imagination.

Remember:
To truly meet means there will not be two entities
meeting, there can only be a unicity, a wholeness.

573

You don't have to bear all of this life. You *are* all of it.
Don't feed yourself so little of yourself.
Eat all of yourself up. Don't ask how.
Just say Yes and swallow.

574

Awareness is the fact. It is the root of being.
To the mind, awareness may appear to be a state.
That would be the fiction.
Awareness is not a state—it is your Self.

575

Which is greater: the bliss that came and went,
or the witness of bliss, which cannot come or go?

576

You are more important than any glimpse,
because without you the glimpse cannot happen,
even if you glimpse God.
And I don't mean you, personally.

577

Truth and awareness are not different. They are one.
But awareness is higher than liberation
because awareness cannot be liberated.
It need only be recognised as that which simply is.

578

Whatever is going to happen, will pass.
Whatever does not happen, cannot pass.
Can you find that in yourself
which does not happen and cannot pass?

579

Don't imagine that the realisation of the Self is an
experience your mind is having or mind can have.
Neither imagine that you can turn the timeless into
time and 'lose' the Self, which in truth is impossible.
Self-realisation is the single Self recognising itself
as timeless and formless awareness.
Here in the heart of this recognition,
whatever is called mind
is nowhere to be found
or even imagined.

580

Many things are because you notice them.
If you don't notice them, they are not.

581

God does not need to be worshipped as 'other'.
God does not acknowledge individuals.
In the dream of life, you can say this is there,
but this is also God's play.
If spirituality means anything,
it is not to end the dream but rather to end the dreamer.
It's not about getting somewhere else in the dream
or upgrading your story.
Get out of bed!

You don't always want to sing a bhajan.
You don't always want to pray.
You don't always have to meditate.
There is something that doesn't have to do
any of these things, except if it feels like it wants to.
Because it cannot be other than what it is.
It cannot be less than what it is.
It cannot be more than what it is, you see.
I am that. I am this one too.
This is where one and one equals one...and nothing.

My love, it's not that the Self becomes easy or simple,
but rather it becomes obvious.

You talk about when you are
in this beautiful state of presence,
but when are you out of it?
And who are you to be 'out' of it?
I don't know if you grasp
the profundity of these questions,
because when you contemplate deeply, the game is up.
Mind is on a countdown.
Such is the marvelousness of the presence of God.

A relationship with a true Master or Guru is not an easy one, but every day it becomes sweeter and more beautiful as your heart and mind open up to Truth. I remember when I met my Master, Papaji, there was also some fear coming up inside, but I knew it was a healthy fear because of the strong attraction and resistance simultaneously being experienced. This was the facing of Grace which could burn the unreal. The Master is the pure reflection of one's own real Being. He doesn't allow any room for your mind-play. Suddenly, in his presence, you feel like you are the 'other'—a stranger to what is natural and true. The shallowness of ego comes up involuntarily and you will feel out of your depth. In that moment, the pain of not being who you truly are becomes unbearable. Now the old tricks are not accepted currency here.

It is like having a pocket full of euros in the middle of the Sahara Desert. There is no value for it and something feels deeply vulnerable. At this defining moment—where you must either run away with your loot of fool's gold or choose freedom—the greatness of the true Master comes into play.

A true seeker feels that deep energetic discomfort within but recognises it to be a great opportunity, a chance for freedom from the tyranny of the false. Though they may be trembling in their socks, they say Yes with full trust and courage and enter the Heart-Master's presence and grace. There is nothing to be afraid of really. In fact, the Master is not the cause of your discomfort. Such presence only exposes the disharmonies of the ego and pulls the seeker into freedom.

586

Often people let their judgements block a gift from
Grace. Grace sends something to assist you, and you
turn away and say, 'I don't want to learn from him,'
or, 'Why does this always happen to me?' You buy into
your brand of projections and miss all the gifts that are
sent to you, saying, 'Life is not easy. Life is so unkind.'

No, it's you who are unkind. It's you who are rough.
It's you who are stupid. Too much energy spent in the
realm of the superficial—therefore all this confusion
comes. You have to open up and be sensitive again
and see that your life is harmonious when not
interfered with by the conditioned mind. The best
way is to turn your face towards your heart again so
that you begin to hear with wisdom—not listening
to chitchat and gossip and nonsense. By avoiding
such tendencies, you discover your true life.

587

The ego is not alive enough to be killed.
It is only a ghost.
It can only be exposed as an apparition,
whereupon it vanishes in the light of true seeing.

588

Seek forgiveness of those whom you have judged.
Keep your heart empty, light, open
and free from all worries and grievances.
Remain quiet inside your being.

589

God is love.
A love that sets you on fire.
This fire is love, wisdom, freedom and joy.
May the whole world be set on fire.

590

When you pray for someone,
don't pray that they satisfy your projections.
Pray that they find their way
to the source as soon as possible.

591

Your Being is going to become a place
where the mind cannot go.
I'm not talking about the mind
in its practical functioning,
I am talking about the demonic mind,
the ego-mind, the psychological and obsessive mind.
Your head will become mind-free, not a mind field.
Being here in satsang,
you must already be experiencing this.
Just like the fish cannot live in the sky,
your egoic mind cannot live
in the ocean of Truth.

592

If there is no interest in the phenomena
that arise in the mind,
they cannot stick or register
themselves in the consciousness.

Like the smell of flowers carried by the wind
leaves no lasting trace,
similarly, nothing can be embedded
in pure awareness.

593

What you are trying to do is already done.
It's just that the spell of disbelief must leave you now.
You have said Yes inside your heart to the Real.
Don't worry. Grace is taking all delusions away.

Contemplate deeply what I am about to say now.
Grasp it and you will be out of the mind trap for good!

You say you are trying very hard to be the presence.
But that which observes the effort to be the presence,
is that making any effort? The flip side of the ego
is pure awareness. Flick over into the awareness
position in which the effort to be the presence is
seen in much the same way as you would watch
a movie of yourself. The one watching the movie
is separate from the image of himself which is
unreal. There is a natural detachment present.

That which is observing the effort, can it be other
than your Self, the living, unchanging source?
Pay attention to yourself as the serene and formless
seer instead of identifying with the frustrated seeker.
Do you feel the difference?

Confirm your reality here as the formless observing.
You are already the 'somewhere' you are trying
to get to. Be clear about this in your heart.
That's it—job done.

595

The value of life will be determined
by the value you place upon yourself, which, in turn,
depends on what or who you believe you are.
When you discover yourself
to be beyond name, form and conditioning,
life sparkles from the inside like a celestial diamond.

596

The sweetness of God's presence
is not tasted through the self-centred mind.
It is not the fruit of personal effort.
It is the fragrance that arises from the hearts
of those whose minds are centred in Truth.

597.

If it requires no effort to breathe,
it requires no effort to be the Self.
Therefore, all efforts and practices are for the mind
and not for the Self, which is perfectly effortless.

598

Lesser things in life you have asked for and received.
How could you ask for Truth and be rejected?

599

Life is not my business, life is my breath.
When you believe you are a person
you feel like life is something you have,
so you try to protect and control it like a business.
But when you recognise your true Self,
it becomes immediately clear
that life is not what you do but what you are.
Like your breath, it is just flowing spontaneously
and you are one with it.
You are aware of it
and you are just flowing along with it,
but you are also beyond it
as unmoving awareness.

600

There is only the limitless Self.
Know that the knowledge of this
and even the knower of this
are only the limitless Self.

601

The Truth is not anything your mind can imagine.
Because, guess what? Your mind won't be there.

602

You say that a wall of separation between you and me
has been falling away and you began feeling more close
to me, but suddenly fear came. This is a very common
phenomenon at this stage in the awakening process.
Something is powerfully attracted to Truth,
but at the same time there arises resistance
to coming closer to the Master.

Heart is attracted to the Heart but the mind says,
'Listen, that's such a bad idea. I don't approve
of this affair. You belong with me.'
The mind feels afraid of me, but it is not afraid of you.
After all, you pay its bills. It will tell you anything and
everything unpleasant so that you don't come near to
me because our relationship threatens its existence.

Mind says, 'I am your personal advisor,
your own personal Google. Whatever your desires,
it is I who helps you to fulfil them.
And now you don't need me anymore?
You just want to be?! Well, we'll see about that!'

But it is all just a mind game going on in the awareness itself. You must clearly see this. Be one with the source where no trouble can come. It is your natural place. Peace and love dwell there.

Your mind does not want you to experience the power that is there when you are alone as Truth itself. It must divert your attention away from the real in order to survive. But your power is greater than all the mind's combined strengths. Only, you must recognise this.

Transcendence is the name of the game.
It is the greatest game on earth.
You are here to win yourself back.
No matter what happens, your attitude should be,
'Yes, I go for gold.'
And don't fight.
Trust and remain as the undivided seer.
Let Grace deal with the mind.

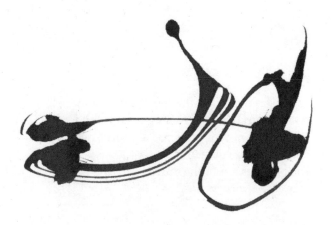

603

Don't be too quick to interpret the moment.
Just keep quiet.
My encouragement is:
Never think anything is against you.
Everything is a blessing.
Why should it be different?
Just be quiet. See how it works itself out.

604

Daily life is the arena in which the wisdom and
experience you claim you have gained are tested.

605

If you do what is right inside your own Heart,
it cannot turn out to be wrong for others. Trust this.

606

The Self is the flower that no one can hold.
It knows itself by recognising what is not itself.
Though the mirror gives you a perfect reflection,
don't look for yourself there.
The power is not in the mirror.
Stay as the witness only.

Whatever experiences may arise, allow them to be expressed. They flow within the human expression of consciousness. Let them be. Because when they have been given the room to express themselves, then the space behind, which is joyful, steady and tranquil, will come to the front. Only don't name this enlightenment or feel that you've gained something. Instead recognise and pay full attention to the unchanging silence which is the substratum of all that is appearing in the mind.

608

What is your highest teaching?

To listen to what comes from my mouth is high,
but higher than that is to put your head in my mouth.

609

The Master says, Die but don't be dead.
But satsang is not to die—it is to kill death itself.
We are not here to make sense.
Did God create this world and say, 'Go and make sense!'?
No, no, no—nothing really 'makes sense'.
And when you know this, everything becomes beautiful.

610

For me, all this life is bullshit.

No, it is not bullshit.
It is holy shit—the best shit in town.
It's not only free, but it sets you free.

611

There is so much power in you when you know
you cannot compromise the Truth inside your heart.
Be willing to lose everything
knowing that which cannot be lost.

612

Mind is not really your enemy;
it will only appear so while you believe you are a person.
Its role is to frustrate your projections,
but in fact what it is really doing is preventing you
from sustaining the delusion
that you are merely a person
—a contracted and inhibited form of consciousness.
Once this is clear for you it will become easy to
recognise and be satisfied in the knowing that you
are unbound awareness, the unborn space
in which the mind itself is perceived.

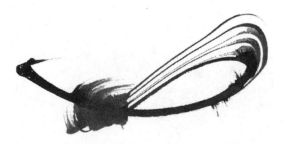

613

Through devotion, surrender and love,
one becomes eternal.
Through Self-knowledge and wisdom,
one becomes timeless.
Contemplate this.

614

All beings love themselves best,
but the sage does not have
this love for a personal self,
for he is without personhood.
The sage simply is,
but his is-ness inspires
love and devotion in the whole world.

615

The one who is seeking to stabilise
in the unchanging Self
is itself a thought watched
from the unchanging Self.

616

Learning takes place in the head.
Understanding takes place inside the heart
and expresses as direct experience.

617

Go inside the cave
of your own heart.
When you can bear and
be your own emptiness,
you are free.

618

You must digest and acknowledge and respect your
seeing. Otherwise you just keep going back and
forth from personhood. Some people attend every
satsang but they don't learn. They just want you to do
something for them. But why don't you just listen?
Then you can do everything for yourself!
I keep putting a mirror in front of you,
but you continue asking, 'How does it work?'
What to do . . .

619

There is not a 'somebody' being empty,
peaceful and aware. There is only emptiness and peace
inside pure immutable awareness.
When the illusion of a seeming 'somebody'
is seen through, the real is revealed.
This Self is not really 'you' at all in the physical,
psychological or historical sense.
It is pure perfection. You are That.

620

It often takes a long time to recognise
the gift already in your hands.

621

Everyone wants something for free
but no one wants freedom.

Sometimes you should stand up and defend what
you know is true. Sometimes we are too attached to
being comfortable. Don't shrink away; this is all the
play of consciousness—to expose that we put our
person first. It's so uncomfortable to stand up and to
have your sense of integrity challenged or to point
the finger or to be disliked or to get into a fight or
to become bright red in front of everybody. And it
could be much worse. I say this is a small price to pay
for freedom and Truth. Sometimes life compels you
to stand up. Even if you are only one against eight
billion, what an amazing thing! You stood for this!

You also have to be willing, in a way, to die
somewhere inside yourself for the principles of the
Heart. I'm not sending you in front of tanks and
machine guns. I'm just telling you to stand up in
your truth as guided by the Heart, even in small
matters. Life gives you a chance to stand up and
live from the Truth that you have discovered.

623

Let the world call you lazy for not running about
like a frightened ghost.
Just be quiet inside yourself.
Don't bother about knowing how things should be
and simply begin observing
without prejudice, projections or desires.
Notice how life flows of its own accord.
Nothing here is a chaos, but a harmony.
Your activities are inside this flow,
but your Self is one with it.

624

There is a gem that is rarely seen in this world.
This gem is one whose heart is free of desire
but is full of love for Truth.
Such a one shines with the light and presence
of the Supreme Lord.
Find him within yourself.

625

The 'I am' is the womb of existence.
Thought itself is the sperm of the being.
When this sperm touches the 'I-me' egg,
the world is born.
When the world is believed to be true,
both the believer and the world come into suffering.
When the womb itself is seen,
the seer is the Unborn.

I am opening the door to true understanding
and direct experience for you.
You have to come out of all delusion
and the biggest one is, 'I am the body and person.
I am the 'thinker' of thoughts and the 'doer' of actions.
I am the giver and receiver.'
Such delusions must vanish altogether.
But we cannot just somehow snap a finger
and come out of delusion
—even if you say it is all you really, really want.
But you have said Yes to Truth even though, at
present, it is not firmly established in your heart.
This Yes is opening doors
in the visible and invisible realms.
Something is being refined by Grace
in order that Truth gets established in the heart.
There is a space there, an unshared space.
Two kings cannot sit on one throne.
You don't have to be a perfect sage
but you have to want the Truth perfectly.
Something perfect and infinite is here,
and I cannot say what it is, for it is wordless.
But work is going on in every heart
to prepare for its coming.
Everyone has to be touched
by the spirit of John the Baptist.
Who is this John?
He is the one who goes ahead to prepare each heart
for the coming of the Holy One.

627

Before true knowledge reveals itself,
ignorance needs to be fully swept aside.
Wisdom will not reveal itself
while there is investment in the unreal,
for that portion of energy will continue
creating divisions and distractions
in order to avoid or delay seeing what truly Is.
Such is the nature of the psychological mind.
Know, it does not exist.

628

How swift it can be to recognise the Truth.
It needn't take weeks, months or years.
This is a hoax. Reject it.
Truth has nothing to do with time.
In fact, it is timeless.
If one's genuine search is for Truth,
know it is already here.

629

The most powerful *sadhana*
is that as you truly see, you are free.
As you understand, you are liberated.
Not that you understand and then practise.
Understand this.
Faster than Zen.

Self-inquiry begins as a method and ends as a mirror,
a mirror in which the timeless perceives its formless reflection.

631

Even when we have been in satsang for a while,
we continue to nurture and protect our individual
identity and the sense of personal autonomy.
You still hold onto this even though you know
it is ephemeral by nature.
And what is the cost of holding onto identity?
It blocks the profound recognition that sets us free.

632

If you put your full attention on consciousness,
it is compelled to open its flower.
When your mind's heart is in the position of Yes,
your absorption is immediate.
Yes means, 'I am open to you, O Supreme Being,
who alone exists. Remove any notion of separation.'

633

If you wish to be happy, no one can stop you.
Similarly, if you wish to be free, no one can stop you.
In fact, the universe encourages
and supports your freedom. Why?
Because to be happy and free is your natural state.

634

God can never be close.
God can never be close because it would mean that there
is some place where God is not. God is infinite.
We cannot exist outside of the infinite.
Therefore, God is our reality.

635

Let the attention move about
—your stillness is undisturbed.
Notice and acknowledge this simple fact.
Then on that day, in that moment
when the mind strikes again,
this fact will remain unchanged,
for you will know
that nothing of significance is happening.
Nothing can alter your being.
Relax in the full joy of this knowing.
Here you are not a traveller on the way to some place,
not even Nirvana.
There are no maps for the omnipresent.
Here you simply are and have always been,
O Limitless One.

636

True love, peace, joy, wisdom and lasting contentment
do not require any effort in themselves. Why?
Because they are the natural fragrances
inside your very nature,
and what is natural is also effortless
and need only be discovered.
Therefore consider:
Beyond a certain necessary stage,
could not your very efforts become an obstacle
to recognising the wholeness
already present inside your heart
—a wholeness that can only be recognised,
not developed?
Seek the Lord's or *Satguru's* grace.

637

I do not desire a life,
a future or anything apart from you,
O Beloved One.

638

If you only sit *with* the Buddha,
you may only develop your *buddhi*.
But if you sit *inside* the Buddha,
you will find the Buddha sitting inside you.
Then you will be one with the Buddha.

639

The Master does not merely tell you verbally about Truth.
He communicates Truth directly and energetically
through his wisdom and gracious presence
into the inner ear or the very bloodstream of Being.
This is the power of a true Master.

640

Though I love you,
do not think I am here to protect the personal 'you',
for Truth as love and wisdom
compels me to drive out those forces
that appear to hold the beingness hostage.
Until you are fully free from their hypnotic grip
you will continue to protect these forces,
believing them to be an integral part of yourself,
and so miss the true power of the Infinite.

641

If you are aware of the Self, then you may enjoy
the person, because it is no threat.
It's like playing with a snake that has no fangs.

642

It is not you who takes care of life.
Life takes care of life.
Find out who you are.
Life is unfolding spontaneously
in the presence of that holy Being.

643

Many times you may hear me say,
When you are speaking,
with what identity are you speaking?
Are you ego, mind, body or presence?
And you have to go back and check in with yourself.
Something we rarely do.
But if you develop the discipline to follow this exercise,
it will exorcise all your troubles.

You have to go beyond
this identification with the body
and the belief in personhood.
Otherwise it is going to kill you.
It will suffocate your spontaneity
and clog up your pure intelligence.
Who amongst us will shake off the ego?
For the one who succeeds,
it won't matter where you go;
only the scenes will change but you, the seer,
remain unchanging.
You will stay untouched
—not by effort or skill or yoga or meditation,
but through perfect understanding
of your true nature confirmed inside the heart.
Grace must be there, but for Grace to reveal herself,
the thirst for Truth must come first.
Arrogance cannot be there.
It may appear in the beginning
but not in the end.
Arrogance cannot be there,
for it is the odour of the devil
and will be swept away
by the power and light of Truth.

Strange as it seems, there is no devil without you.
As an ego, you are the devil's accomplice.
If you divide yourself, delusion will seep in
through your most available weakness.

646

Truth often shows up
when it seems inconvenient to the mind,
but its ways are ever perfect.

647

Sometimes I say to God, 'Father, forgive me.'
And He laughs at me.
Like, why do you say such things? You love me.
Your love for me makes everything you do righteous.

648

Beloved, you are both the invitation
and the response to come Home.

649

The Self has no intentions,
not even the intention to kill the ego.
For the Self, ego does not exist.

650

Sometimes, you feel you're fighting against the
unknown, but you *yourself* are the unknowable.
Reflect. You are only believing in the apparent
known. To know what is coming is not the purpose
of life. We only have this obsession when we are
deluded. When you are happy, you don't think about
future. You don't think about anything actually.
You only think about past and future when you are
not happy. Don't buy into this. Don't buy into any
state. Stay as the stateless. Simply remain empty.

651

When you are looking from your true place, the
psychological role of the mind has accomplished
its mission. It has done what it can do. It helps
you home by exposing the false in you. It helps
you home, and nobody says thank you.

652

When Truth is discovered,
the eyes drop their promiscuity
and become unified in the single seer,
the Self Supreme.

653

The one who is without 'with' alone is.

654

I am not a moral man, it's just that I am never going
to accept you or trust you or believe your story or take
your side or be your friend or accept your promises and
believe in your vows until you truly discover and be the
Self you fully are. For until your breath and presence
smell of God, and your face shines with the light of
his presence, your existence will be merely a play of
transience—fleeting ingenuineness. Only when the face
of time and matter fades away, leaving the timeless face
of the Supreme, will I bow at your feet with all my heart.

655

Who knows the exquisite joy that shines
in the heart of the awakened mind?
You will know once you cease identifying
with what you are not.

656

Nothing belongs to you or me. Nothing belongs.
Everything, everything, everything simply is.

657

You have to become the tiger,
and the ego must be in your teeth.

658

You don't know how well you are doing;
you don't know anything at all.
You are just a baby in God's lap.

659

Don't be measuring yourself
by the standard of your thoughts.

660

For a while, the mind strives for understanding the
Truth. But as soon as the Truth actually becomes
imminent, at that very point where one is about
to flower into freedom, mind begins to back pedal,
fighting for its very existence. Its former earnestness
for Truth is replaced with riotous resistance, and
unexpectedly a mutiny to sink the ship of freedom
surfaces. Though it may seem that you are at
your weakest point, you are actually at the edge
of victory! Don't panic. Keep quiet and remember
you are one with God. This battle will end here.

661

The mere fact that you are here with me
is evidence of your impending dissolution.

662

Shiva fever is different from other fevers.
Something inside is burning, crackling,
but know you are being pulled up by Grace.
You can be cooking inside your sleeping bag,
but inside your heart is total serenity and joy.
Empty.
Outside: crispy and crackling.
Inside: complete serenity, limitless space.
You are being emptied from the inside out.
No longer are you merely a wave
on the surface of your boundless ocean.
Everything is purified and whole.
Your eyes are calm and clear again.

663

Once the consciousness truly catches hold of
its own root and begins digesting and confirming
its own recognition, its true seeing,
there is no turning back.
The world, the sense of personhood, of 'I' and 'other'
—the whole thing collapses.
You have crossed over.
You are genuinely cured of the delusion of personhood.
You come to an end of effort, separation and practice.
It's hard to convince the world that It, the real Self,
is there before practice.
How can you practise to be what you already are?
The trouble is that people don't really know they are That.

664

It is not the person, but the consciousness that wakes
up from this mess, and when it wakes up,
it realises this so-called mess is divine.

665

The true bliss of the Self is the only real ecstasy there is.
It is not a narcotic that will stupefy your mind
or create any delusion.
It is completely natural.
It is synonymous with Truth and Being.
Seek it with all your mind and heart.

666

I am both that which is permanent
and that which seems to be impermanent and
moving. But I am neither absolutely.
That which witnesses both
but itself is uncaused and unseen
—That I Am.

667

Of ourself, we are the last to be aware.
We cannot not be aware,
but you are not aware that you are aware.
When you are aware that you are aware, you are free.

668

*Mooji, please help me to be brave enough to leap into
the vastness that you seem to speak from. I'm so afraid
of failure.*

More than forcing yourself to be brave, more important
than that is to inquire into yourself. You still have
to be an 'I' to be brave. Look at who is going to be
brave, and look at who might fail. When you look at
bravery, do you see emptiness needing to be brave
or somethingness being brave? Just keep looking
and looking and see that behind all these changeful
things, you are unaffected. With such understanding,
all thoughts immediately lose their virility.

669

Few people can grasp the Truth as it really is.
They grasp it intellectually,
but when it is grasped in the heart
or it grasps you in the heart,
no separation can persist.
There can be no 'you' and it; there is only Truth.
The grip of God suffocates the ego.
In the light of Truth, ego cannot live further as
separation and merges into the One.

670

The lovers of God never think of
themselves as special or great,
knowing all greatness is Him alone.
Casting themselves aside,
only He remains in the heart as the Supreme Self.
There is neither duality nor non-duality
for him who is beyond all.

671

I know you and love you far too much
to treat you as a mere person.

672

As a person, you are fiction.
The only fact is the Self.

673

If there was a sage who wished to impart his highest
teaching to you, then he would have to get you to a
place beyond your mind in order for you to receive
it. And I don't mean beyond in any kind of spatial
way, because what I am referring to has no space to be
other than here. Everything else is a visitor. Even the
state of presence is a visitor, but That—the Real—is
not a visitor, and it is not visited either. It simply is.
It cannot depart, nor can it arrive.
Even to say 'it reveals itself'
is only because of the limitation of language.
It cannot be conveyed through words alone.

You, as a person, are like a face drawn in the sand.
It is there, but the sand knows nothing about it.
We can draw a picture in the sand as great as a Picasso or
a Michelangelo but the desert neither loses nor gains any
grains. It is neither happy nor sad to meet you.
The desert does not know or remember you.
The one who draws, the stick and material used,
the drawing itself and the perceiving of it
—all are expressions of one wholeness.
We are that Oneness.

674

You are not going to become the Truth.
You are going to unbecome the lie.

675

When the flower opens, the bud disappears.

676

When one is able to observe even the state of presence
whereby the state of presence becomes itself
phenomenal to a deeper seeing,
one is automatically, effortlessly,
in the state of the absolute Being.

677

Don't think 'I am',
Be 'I am'.

678

It is only when you sit truthfully inside your Self
that you can be truly generous in your expression.
And you find you are not being generous
—life itself becomes the manifestation of
generosity when the ego is no more.

679

Don't know anything at all.
Meet everything in the moment as it arises.
Meet life like this and you are on the road to
true and pure existence,
everlasting joy and contentment.
Then your life is not a series of events,
but more a quality of being.
Start with being empty before you make your first step.
Then, when you make your first step,
see if you leave this beautiful emptiness or not.
When you are so grounded in and as the source,
it won't matter if you make one, ten or a hundred steps
—in any direction, they will still be steps
made in the silence of being.
The one who follows my advice
will find something truly worth discovering.
Discovering yourself as you truly are
is discovering life as it truly is.

680

All of life is only consciousness falling under the spell
of its own projections and then drawing
on its deepest powers to remember itself.
Say Yes to the inner prompting.
This will be your clue that auspiciousness
has awakened within you.

681

Beloved, all that you perceive here is impermanent.
Therefore, don't try to make heaven on earth or
with earth. Find the real heaven inside you
—a heaven that will never decay.

682

We don't need to be afraid of the world.
We are not the police
that we would approach anybody with suspicion.
Here in the *sangha*, even if a thief comes,
we welcome them and offer them a glass of water.
Let your first expression be one of openness
and welcome and love and not suspicion.
God's way is . . . welcome.

683

The love you know is bound.
The love you don't know is eternally free.
You cannot capture it.
It captures you and transforms you into love.
Will you take that risk? Trust your Master.
When this happens, there will only be One.

684

Except for answering the call of nature,
a devotee, student or disciple should avoid leaving
the Master's presence during his discourse.
In fact, I would rather you wet yourself
than miss your Self.

Just now, leave aside this conviction that you
are bound. In fact, why not also leave aside the
belief that you are free. Why? Because one's real
Self is there before belief or conviction. This is
naturally undeniable. The true Self requires neither
belief nor conviction in order to be itself.

It is not a person. It is beyond thought. Find out
who seeks to be convinced. Really try to identify
the one who makes all these claims. One's Self
and Truth are synonymous. They are one.
Not holding onto anything, including the sense
of 'I-me', observe and be that which remains.

If one recognises Truth as Truth,
from where does the power come
to discern the real from the unreal?
And who or what is experiencing this discovery?
I am genuinely asking this.
Please respond.

Why do people say,
'Thank you for allowing me to be nobody'?
Because to be somebody is a burden.
Here alone, in the presence of the real,
one recognises the effortlessness of being.

688

Without the light of the sun, nothing can be seen.
Light is the greatest sculptor.
It reveals the forms of all things.
Salutations to the sun.
Without the light of consciousness, neither the sun,
 nor its light nor anything else can be seen.
Salutations to consciousness.
Without you, where is the world?
Without you, what would perceive the play of existence?
In satsang, you are introduced again and again
to consciousness, which is your own light.
You come to the recognition that consciousness itself
is the source of all manifestation and that without
it, nothing can be perceived to exist.
You are both consciousness and simultaneously
the perceiver of consciousness. Are you aware of this?
Without you, the perceiver of consciousness,
neither consciousness nor its content exist.
The universe *is* . . . because you *are*.

Intimate moments, Swami Swatantranand Ashram, Rishikesh, India 2016

Opening ceremony at the Christ Chapel, Monte Sahaja, Portugal, August 2016

A moment of quiet reflection in the Christ Chapel, Monte Sahaja, Portugal 2016

Just Keep Quiet

The Truth is not going to be anything that you can perceive in front of yourself and at some distance away. It is always the subject, never an object. Take subject and source to be one. Therefore, don't keep looking at what is seen, but instead bring your attention to that from where the seeing emerges. Note that the seeing position is not trapped inside the bubble of the objects perceived. To whom is all this occurring? Is it to a person, some tangible entity that can be recognised? Can that in whose presence even the functioning of perception is perceived, can this itself be recognised phenomenally? And if so, by whom or what? Do you follow?

If you have been following my pointing diligently, you will be able to answer directly from the Self. Who or what are you? Look, feel and confirm. Your sincere introspection will have caused mind to burn up all its concepts. It will have nothing more to offer. What is left now?

Myself.

Don't use anyone else's words or findings now. Rely on your own discovery. Don't identify with anything new.

Don't pick up any more concepts.

There is just this.

This what?

It is formless and indefinable.

Yes. This is the Self. It is not other than you. Like this, you have come to the end of words. Very good.

Now just keep quiet.

689 Such blessedness, for I am never separated.
I am the indivisible one, the inexhaustible.
This great world is just a mighty mirror
that God put in front of me
that I may taste the joy of seeing His face.
I know nothing about living life. I am life.
I have done nothing.
I just am.

The body may get weary and fatigued,
but the spirit is ever free and full of light and love.
This is blessedness.
Such a privilege I have.
Such things I have seen while moving
in the craft of this body, such bliss.
God is always walking in us
but blessed is the moment when we come to see this.
Rejoice in that inside your heart.
Melt in this love.
I am the awareness
in which my Father's reflection is seen.
How to say such things...will anyone take offence?
I am the light of this world.

690 Thought, imagination and belief have created a 'me'.
I wonder whose belief it is.
Obviously the one who wonders.
And who is that? Obviously, the one who asks.
And who knows that...

691

There is an innocence in you
that all the Saints and Prophets
of all times and of all religions
are tirelessly pointing to.
It is perfect and can never be lost.
Though for many it appears to be hidden,
it can never be altered or destroyed,
for there is nothing apart from itself.
It can only appear to be masked
by the belief in personal identity and conditioning.
Through the urge for real understanding,
the false is now being exposed,
undone and replaced by the truth.
Come to this altar
with a heart of full devotion and openness.
Offer up yourself in service to the imperishable
and keep quiet.

692

I am speaking on behalf of you. I am your confidence.
I am you in confidence, speaking to you,
unafraid to say what I am and what you are.
It is possible. It is done.
I am everlasting freedom itself.

693

You rebel against your parents' expectations
for they wish you to become what you are not.
I also have an expectation of you:
I expect you to be only what you truly are.
But this too you rebel against—that which sets you free.

694 *ƒ*
First come out of the dream of *maya*.
Then later you may go in again, if you wish to.
You can enjoy the dream while being awake.
Thus, free of delusion,
the one who is awake
enjoys this dream
the most.

695 *ƒ*
You say the mind gets in the way of finding
the Truth. This is simply not true.
Nothing can 'get in the way' of the true,
for Truth is not to be found in any direction.
It is always present as the core of your being.
For anything to be 'in the way',
you must be trying to get to some place
other than where you already are.
Nothing can stop you from finding Truth.
You are not going anywhere to be stopped.
Truth is discovered right where you are.
Let us be clear about this.

696 *ƒ*
It is the greatest miracle that a human being,
born with so many challenges,
can rise like the lotus flower above the water.
It grows in a muddy place
but remains immaculate throughout its life.
Even if the rain falls heavily and the waters rise,
the lotus will still be always above the surface.
This is the nature of the spirit.

You say you have heard stories about being swallowed
by the Master and so you became afraid of me.
But now you say it is different.
Your only wish is to disappear completely.
Therefore don't touch or combine yourself
with anything at all. Just be open.
Now the real Master, the *Satguru* within,
is going to swallow you from inside.
This means your mind is being merged
in the universal Heart.
It is all unfolding by itself naturally.
And it is the most beautiful thing.
Don't listen to what the mind has to say now.
Stay only in the experience itself.
Don't imagine.
Keep quiet.
Without expectations,
you will feel the presence stirring within you.
No sense of specialness.
No arrogance.
No pride.
Such joy.
Such peace.
Just the natural Being.
Welcome home

698

Surrender your existence to existence.
Discover your spontaneity.
To entertain the belief that you know what you are going
to do in the future or next week is a madness.
What restriction and repression.
Life flows spontaneously and is infinitely greater
than all your plans or intentions put together.
Why spoil it with hasty and vain projections?
Let it be whatever it will be.
Give up trying to manipulate.
This is freedom.

699

Many people feel either it is their destiny to realise the
Self or not. But the Self has no destiny. Boom! Who is
saying, 'If it is in my destiny to discover the Self, it will
happen?' This one is not real. If you would really listen to
what I am saying and what I am pointing to, you would
save yourself lifetimes of effort and suffering. However,
if you have a secret commitment to preserving yourself
as a person, self-inquiry will not help you. You have
to put everything on the table of Truth. You cannot
surrender and have something hidden behind your back.

700

The field of the mind is unending.
You cannot come to the end of mind.
It's like an unending mandala, and none of it is real.
You cannot make a fact out of an illusion.

701

How beautiful and rare to find one who is free of
intentions, desires and needs—one who has come
to that state which is not driven by the urge to
control existence or to become anything. One's
mind comes to a beautiful place of openness, silence
and peace. In fact, one does not create such a state;
one simply stops identifying with the projections
of the conditioned mind and so comes to recognise
and be established in one's original nature.

702

You say you don't want your person anymore.
You are tired of it, you say.
And all you want is for it to leave you alone.
You, who says this, is who?
Clarify this.
Is the pure awareness, the Self, saying these things?
Look into it now.
Who is so disturbed?
The one who says, 'I want the person to leave me alone,'
leave that one alone and stay as the voiceless One.

703

I don't need to teach you this.
It is enough that I show you your own door.
And when you open it,
you will find you are already inside.

704

You cannot find the Self like you find a missing torch.
It is not that type of finding.
To find your Self, you must leave everything else.
That is why I say it is sublimely simple.
Of course, sometimes fear comes,
'I don't know if I can afford to lose all this.'
Well, do you really *have* anything?
If you really have something,
why would you be afraid to lose it?
If it can be lost, it is not really yours. It belongs to
time. If it is true, then it cannot be lost.
Therefore, value only the real—your formless Being.

705

For a long time we have been measuring activity
mainly in physical terms. But there are some
beings whose energy and presence powerfully
impact upon the life flowing around them, yet
they are not necessarily engaged in activity. They
impart peace, wisdom and the joy of being with
a mere glance. And yet they unhesitatingly
confess to knowing and doing nothing at all.

706

I am only speaking of you.
This is the Self.
It is not afraid of life;
it is not afraid of death.
It is not afraid.
It just is.
Whatever direction you take,
the sunlight is the same.
The sun does not have a back or a face.
Every angle, every part is good.
Every part of your Self as awareness is good.
Everything about you is holy.

707

The climate of your being is always open, quiet and
kind. Of course there is room for a little fire now
and again, but it won't burn your house down. Give
everything a little space. No need to be a traffic
policeman on some mental motorway. Let all come
and go, but you stay as you are. Like this, harmony
prevails. This is self-love in its truest expression.

708
You must win yourself back
from the psychological identity.
I will fight for you but only if you are willing
and ready to fight for yourself.
I won't fight instead of you.

709
Make use of your time to evict personal tendencies
and habits. True spirituality is not about making you
feel comfortable with your projections. You have to
be thoroughly clean. I don't mean squeaky clean, like
you only have good thoughts and no desires, but that
you use everything life brings you to confirm the
Truth. Be the space where all expressions arise, play
and then exhaust themselves without confusing you.
Any moment and from any direction, look and find
your unmoving Self. This is spiritual maturity.

710
This body's wellness or unwellness
has nothing to do with my state of being.
My joy is untouched.

711
What is greater than wealth? Gratitude.

712

Your mind says, 'Come with me, follow me.
I take you to God. I know where he is.'
Believing this, you go on a journey to find the one
from whom you have never been apart.

713

How are you going to understand Truth?
To study and read holy scriptures is not enough.
Better than mechanical study of the scriptures,
go and drown yourself in the Master's spit.
Your heart has to be baptised in the spirit of God
—in full trust and openness.
Then alone will intuitive
and effortless knowledge
awaken in you.

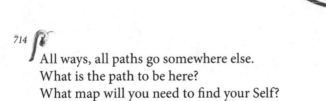

714

All ways, all paths go somewhere else.
What is the path to be here?
What map will you need to find your Self?

715

In the Heart of each and every Being, I Am.

716

Higher than remembering God
is to completely dissolve in God.

717 *

Do not hold onto any concept,
   even the most beautiful concept.
   Just stay empty. This is your wellness, your true health.
   You are simply here,
   not waiting, neither coming nor going.
   Neither in nor out. These are mere references.
   Don't pick up any concept.
   If there is any tightness in the body
   or restlessness in the mind,
   it is only a sensation,
   it is only a tightness or a restlessness
   —it is not a reading of what you are.

718 *

For a true seeker, the question 'Who am I?'
   when engaged with deeply,
   will so molest their straying tendencies
   that their mind is left with no other choice
   than to rest inside their own heart
   as what they cannot not be.

719 *

Forget about remembering or forgetting yourself.
   These are only for your mind. Why all this trouble?
   Just stay as the Self.

720 *

There is nowhere left for me to go but to be with You.

721 ♪ Yourself without you is the face of God.

722 ♪ You say, 'The Truth is uncatchable.'
Do you know why It is uncatchable?
Because the one who says
that It cannot be caught does not exist.
Truth is already here, but something, a voice,
is referring to Truth as 'It'.
But is there really something other than It
to be able to refer to It as 'It'?
Or is It itself referring to itself as 'It'?
Because if you feel there is something else
called 'a person' referring to It as 'It',
you will never find It. It will always be a theoretical 'It'.
But when it is found that It alone exists,
and only It can call itself 'It',
then . . . that's It!

723 ♪ My love, having discovered your inexhaustible
infinite Self, why would you want to go back
and live in the tiny cupboard of your ego?

724 ♪ Demons live in the past and future.
Gods exist in the now.
The Sage is Timeless.

Live cradled in the lap of God.

Your soul is flying away from definitions,
and the mind feels unbearable.
Don't keep thinking something is wrong with you.
This is an investment from the mind itself,
and it will interpret every single thing,
even a lump in the throat, as something wrong,
'I feel so blocked.' It will do this.
Somebody has a burning kneecap,
'Oh yes! This is stopping me.'
It's not! Nothing is stopping you.
Nothing takes you away from who you are,
except through imagination—that's it!
There is no other way it can happen,
because it's not true.
You are eternally yourself, the rest is only a dream.
This is why it is called awakening.

Being here with me is for liberation. No other reason.
It is not to spiritualise or save the planet, nor to set up a
group with an exclusive identity, nor to run away from life.
I'm not interested in any of that. Of course, everything has
its place; everything is the play of consciousness. But I'm
not interested in aspirations inside consciousness, because
however beautiful, it is all ephemeral. Please don't be shocked
by this. Your Self is beyond all of that. No pain there, because
it is beyond the field of interrelated opposites. Go all the way.
A true one goes all the way.

728 There comes a time when you will be unable to look and find anything that is you. There will also come a time when you will be unable to look and find anything that is *not* you. This is a great mystery... but for whom?

729 Christians claim that Jesus
died on the cross to give us everlasting life.
But it wasn't on the cross that he died to save mankind.
It was at his baptism that he died to save your life.
He died to himself during the temptation in the
wilderness—he overcame his person so that the true light
that could heal humanity would enter the world. Such
is the power that shines in the absence of the ego.
He exchanged himself in order to serve God
and to be with God alone.
And that is how he is saving you today.

730 ❧
Only when I perceive love within you do I have the
feeling that I know you. When your presence emits the
perfume of openness, compassion, gratitude and silence,
there comes a natural feeling of being in the presence of
holiness. We start remembering who we are. We feel we
are looking at God's face—bathing in his presence. Then
the sense of a deep recognition appears inside the heart
and everyone begins to feel at home. If I don't perceive
this in your presence, I simply don't see you at all.

731 ❧
I am here *for* freedom
has to become I am here *as* freedom.

732 ❧
I have not come to burden you. In fact, I have come
to unburden you from all this needless suffering.
The divine is not one millimetre away from you.
You have tried it your way, now try it my way.

733 ❧
All our life, our birth, our death
has been spent in the ocean.
Unexpectedly something comes along and says,
'You imagine this water life is all there is, but you
are a bird. Look at your wings. You belong to the
sky, like me. It is time to leave the water.'

734

You say you want to drop the 'I',
but the 'I' cannot drop the 'I'.
There must be something
that is not the 'I' to drop the 'I'.
It is That which is aware of 'I',
the most holy concept, the immaculate concept.
Be That in which the 'I' itself arises.
Then you don't have to drop the 'I'.
You don't have to drop anything.
You don't have to kill anything.
You don't have to heal anything.
You don't have to fix anything.
You don't have to become anything
or unbecome anything.
You don't have to work on anything.
You don't have to evolve.
You cannot evolve to go back to what you are.
Have I gone too far?
This guidance is for the one who wishes to be
conscious of their own consciousness right now.
If you intend to awaken next year,
we have to go back to 'I' which is time and change.

735

As mind merges inside the heart,
true understanding awakens.
You are the invisible inside the visible,
the unmoving inside all movements.
Like space moving in space
glowing inside a thin skin called a human being.

736 *Sometimes the old mind will come and say,
'Aha! Brilliant! Okay, now you're ready to share...'
But you stay here.
When I say 'stay here' it does not mean don't move, ·
but remain here, in the silence of being.
When you are here, your body will do what is needed,
but the idea that you are distracted from awareness
or taken out of your Self will become meaningless;
you will come to see that nothing
can remove you from awareness
because awareness is what you are.
You will notice that some listening occurs,
some speaking occurs, some movement occurs,
but something is not occurring—you are this.

737 *Human beings should be the living embodiments
of the Supreme. Everything else we have tried. We
have all the comforts. We have invented them for our
pleasure and have tasted them all. Still we are not
happy. Because only one thing can satisfy the heart,
and that is to be free of the delusion of egoic identity,
and to fall in love again with the Supreme. Here you
cannot stay apart as a lover, for you are now so fully
absorbed that there remains nothing but the Indivisible.

738 *The most simple appears to be the most difficult.
Difficulty itself is an illusion.
Simple also is an illusion.
Disregarding these, what remains?

Sometimes the presence of the Lord is too much.
You try to go to bed but the bed rejects you.
Sleep rejects you.
Sleep says, 'Go. I don't want you now.
Go and stay with Him. Go and be with your Lord.
Keep the Lord's company. This night you will not sleep.'
Sometimes we are on fire like this
and no water can quench this fire.
You find yourself leaving your house.
You step out under the moonlight,
under the stars to try and cool off
and it is not happening.
It even gets more intense.
You are full of the brightness of the spirit.
This body is made for the holy spirit.
Not for alcohol spirit, but for holy spirit.
You have to drink God's 'Rum Punch'.
When you are drunk in the holy spirit you will forget
everything except him. This is freedom itself.
The house of sorrow is burning
and only the clear space of God is left.
Only That cannot be burnt.

740

Life is inviting you: Slow down in me.
Move in me, with me, as me
in this holy oneness.

741

All aspirations, battles and victories are confined
to the realm of the waking and dream states only,
which is the realm of dynamic consciousness.
Pervading and yet beyond
the waking state and its activities
lies unborn awareness—our true Self.

742

Your eyes are the windows through which I
can gaze into the heart of God.
My eyes are the mirror in which you can see
God reflected inside your own being.

743

When you realise the truth of who you are,
your whole life becomes religion.
Your very existence becomes service
to the one Self, to Truth, to God.

744 Harmony works on every level, but this is something that is difficult to explain. There is only the great harmony. This is why beings on every level are reasonably okay at whatever stage they are. Even apparent disharmony is an aspect of the great harmony. Disharmony is perceived from a position where there is a desire to do something which is not in accord with the universal flow. Then there arises a seeming conflict, which itself is unavoidable and necessary and also a part of the harmony's expression. So absolute is the great harmony that there is space for even apparent disharmony to be expressed without affecting the magnificence of the great harmony. Everything, even seeming disharmony, is in service to the great harmony. In the realm of being, disharmony plays as the person; harmony expresses as pure presence. There is only the one indivisible Self manifesting as the great harmony.

745 You don't need to be special.
You need only to be true.

746 🎷
Be aware of this persistent feeling that there is
something more to do in order to attain the Self.
Somehow, you have been brought to a stage where you
are encouraged to leave aside all intentions, projections
and fantasies, and to simply keep quiet inside your being.

Mind is inclined to say this is not enough. It is
suggesting you take some action. However, the Master
tells you to keep quiet and to focus on the silence of
your Heart rather than the rush of the mind. You are
advised to avoid the sense of waiting for something
to happen. There may arise a little tension because of
this advice to not go with the movements of the mind.
Learn to bear your own silence by observing the
tensions encircling it. Observe rather than react.
Again, keep quiet. Stay only as awareness.

747 🎷
Mostly, we are experiencing
from the state of personhood
and not from our true state.
Crisis helps us to find Christ,
our inmost being.

748 🎷
You cannot enter the heart of purity while holding onto
the unclean ego. You simply cannot do it. It's like trying
to dry yourself off while standing under a waterfall.

749

All of God's gifts are perfectly attuned
to support your awakening—perfectly auspicious.
Don't go by the size but by the potency.
An attitude of gratitude opens your eyes and heart
to make the best use of these gifts.

750

A thought comes and says, 'This is too much.
I just cannot go on.' Who is saying this thing?
It is also perceived. Why must it be believed?
It is enough that it is perceived.
Don't identify with that voice.
It's the same guy again.
Don't identify with that voice.
It is not your true guide.

751

When we have an ego, there is a fear of
losing the identity through awakening.
When we awaken, there's fear that
the ego-self may return.
When we are liberated, fear is no more.

752

Pay attention: when the heart is empty of
intention, it is also empty of tension. And
a heart free of tension blesses the whole world.

The ego is fired but he keeps showing up for work.
We have to get used to him coming and going,
and in some way we should not mind this subtle
tension, because to mind it too much brings you
back into the person. It brings back something that
can be disappointed, which is not the pure Self.

The ego cannot live without interest from you,
without identification, which came because
you were distracted from your true state.
Some subtle tension will always be there
which will keep exercising your spiritual muscle.

Somebody once asked my Master,
'Papaji, you often talk about vigilance,
but in your case, do you have to be vigilant?'
And he said, 'To my very last breath.'
This vigilance is not a job.
It is a joy.

Whenever the mind goes out to something
you simply stay in a state of Self-remembrance
—let the attention rest here.

754   Don't keep picking up the mind.
To find Truth, you must go
beyond mind's influence now.
That inmost place is too sacred
for the shameful mind to bear.
It is an unshared place.
Only Truth dwells here,
and the one who is without ego.
They are one.

755   You can say that our body-mind functioning is destined.
Jesus Christ himself says, 'Not one hair of your head
falls to the ground outside of the will of God.'
Have you heard this before?
But the body-mind functioning is not you.
You are not the hair that will fall to the ground
nor are you the body or the thinking mind.
You are the witness of all of this.
To not know this is to fall under the spell of destiny.
To know this is to be free.

756   A true devotee will find the Master even if
he lives in the belly of the earth itself.

757 To awaken to the timeless and perfect Truth, don't put
so much importance on study. Avoid the tendency
to collect a lot of information on spirituality.
Instead, dive within with your entire heart by saying,
'Yes, I am here for this alone. Drown me in You.'
Information and mind-created knowledge
is meaningless in the higher realm.
Here, only harmony prevails.
By going beyond the notion of a personal self,
the detached observer of all phenomena is discovered
as a formless field of inner silence and harmony.
It spontaneously becomes self-evident
that this is our real nature and position.
This clarity of seeing and understanding arises from
the synchronicity of 'I' with the universal consciousness.
Pure harmony is the language and vibration of
holiness. It is synchronicity with God.

758 How must one come to this altar of nothingness?
You have to come more naked than naked. Empty.
At least have this attitude inside your heart.
In actuality 'you' personally cannot accomplish it,
but your attitude is good enough when you say,
'Yes. Yes, take me all the way.'
Don't give God some checklist of what you want.
Simply be willing to exchange yourself for the Truth.

759   You are timelessly free.
You are already the Self now,
but you must recognise this deep inside your heart.
Don't listen to the devious mind,
for he has never really served the Truth.
You have to strike him at his root now.
Put the axe at the root and cut him out.
Feel no compassion for the unreal,
for he is busy arranging a womb for your next birth.

760   Die to identity... but don't inform anyone.
Save yourself a lot of trouble.

761   How will you be free if you are still living from the
past? Mind and form have past, for they are of time.
Real life springs from emptiness and is ever fresh.
Hold no idea about how things should be.
All must be seen to come from emptiness.
You also must be empty of yourself.
Be emptiness appearing in the form of a human being.

Leave the realm of names and forms
and enter a more refined and intuitive field.
See with Krishna's eyes and love with Christ's heart.
Inquire with Shiva's wisdom and come to the
dimension behind thought, the realm of being.
Here shines the intuitive presence 'I am'.
All beings naturally love this 'I am' state.
Its nature is peace, joy, wisdom and love.
It is the love to be—the love to exist.
But at a certain stage,
even this wonderful state is observed.
When you are in the position to observe the 'I am' itself,
then you are automatically in the place of the unborn.
It is the Supreme One.
No words can convey or define it.
It imparts light and joy to life.
Papaji was once asked,
'Is there anything beyond awareness?'
Surprisingly, he said, 'Love. Love is beyond all.'
Love gives emptiness to emptiness, makes it perceivable.
I have found love to be synonymous with awareness.
They are one.
Yet, paradoxically, they are both beyond each other.
Love is the unity of being.
It is the sacredness within emptiness.
It is the ineffable one.
You are That.

763

Suppose I were to say to you, Since meeting my
Master I have not said anything, I have not done
anything at all, I have not spoken to anybody. You
say, 'What are you talking about? You are always
talking, you have made so many videos.' Would
you understand this type of thing? Talking but not
talking. Teaching but not teaching. Changing but
not changing. No need to say so much about these
things. Perhaps one day I will hear you say them.

764

'I know' is the restless place for all beings.
'I don't know' is the resting place for all beings.

765

Before Adam ate the apple in the garden of Eden,
he was probably in the same state which you are in
right now—the state of Grace.

The fall from Grace is the eating of the apple
from the tree of the knowledge of good and evil.
That fruit is called 'I'. You have heard the saying,
'The apple of my 'I' (eye).' [*Mooji laughs*]
We have not understood it. Adam calls it an apple
—that apple is the belief, 'I am the body.' When this
'I'-apple was eaten, the world fell into darkness.

766 How can you be any thing? Things are only things.
They come and they go. If you are a thing, when it
goes, you also would be gone. But you witness these
comings and goings. Who are you, the one who remains
effortlessly? Contemplate. Can this one be found?
The answer that you cannot find—this is your Self.

767 Do this: disidentify and tell me if there is other
than the perfect. Where is even enlightenment or
ignorance, bondage or freedom, heaven or hell? Even
without denying the phenomenal world and the
play of the senses, one transcends all states of mind
and is immediately free from the grip of desires and
attachments. When deployed, this understanding
is going to detonate and blow all stupidities away.

768 Some falsely imagine that Self-realisation is the
highest state within the phenomenal realm, but this
is not so. The realisation of the Self reveals one's
true position as the unfathomable, beyond even the
concept of Self-realisation. The fully awakened one
has transcended the illusion of duality, of cause and
effect as a fact. They have surpassed the distractions
and temptations of phenomenality. They are one with
the concept-free totality as indivisible awareness.

Having revealed within me
the impermanence of all things,
now absorb me in You forever.

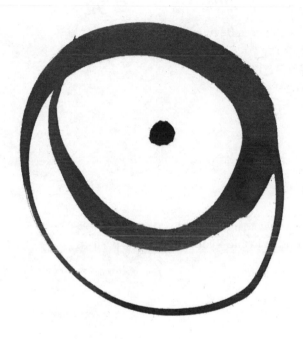

770

May all those who come to meet You through me
fully wake up from the hypnosis of the ego-mind
and realise the imperishable Self.

771

Don't be in you. Be in me.
When we are one, I put you back in you,
to be you without you.
Complete.

772

That on the outside—you do—is good.
That on the inside—you don't do—is perfect.

773

This love and life are not different.
This love and God are not different.
This love and consciousness are not different.
This love and the Absolute are not different.

774   Don't try to change the world.
First, change yourself, or rather your self-perception,
and you find the world automatically corresponding
to the level of your understanding.
You will find that it has always been you
who set the pace and depth of your experience
by recognising and honouring your true nature.

775   Noisy mind, no mind, never mind, same-same.

776   The final bridge to cross is to let go
of the mind-created 'spiritual' self.
Burn that bridge behind you.
Stay empty of self-image and cease looking back.
Remain in the neutrality of being. That's it.

777

We are here to discover this together,
to remind you that there is something within you
that can never be polluted.
It can never go wrong.
It can never be destroyed.
It can never belong to the devil.
It can never die.
You cannot damage it.
You cannot improve it because it is always perfect.
And to help you to find it, to recognise it, simply open
up to its presence. It is not different from you.

778

It could be said that the real spiritual journey
is from the head to the Heart.
However, the Heart does not know
any distance or journeys.
It is only the head that imagines
such things as journeys, trips, tricks and traps.
And I am so happy when one sees that one's true Self
has always been perfectly happy, peaceful and complete.
It is the greatest mystery in the world,
but I wonder... for whom?

779

If you simmer down the highest teachings on Truth,
the quintessence is: Stay as awareness.

780

You are the peace in silence.
You are the silence in peace.
You are the light of consciousness revealing all.
You are the perceiving love, devoid of objective identity.
You are the wisdom and love
that shines from the source of existence.
You are Unborn Awareness Self.

781

Beloved,
Honour your recognition of the Truth
as revealed through Grace.
Digest and assimilate it deeply inside your heart
until it becomes as effortless and as natural
as your own breath.
This is true self-respect, real *sadhana*.
Otherwise, out of habit, it becomes just another thing
you file away in the mind's department of philosophy.
And another chance is missed.

Remember:
Your life is auspicious.
You are here for much more than knowledge.
You are here for Liberation.

782

I Am—before the idea that I could forget myself
or that I needed to remember myself was believed.

Nothing IS

To utter such a
statement
One must first
Be nothing

Glossary

Advaita Non-dual, not two; this oneness is a fundamental quality of everything. Everything is a part of and made of one non-dual consciousness.

Advaitin A spiritual seeker of Truth whose nature is more inclined towards understanding through the wisdom pointings of Advaita.

Bhajan An Indian devotional practice, prayer and hymn to the divine.

Bhakta Beings whose search for Truth expresses through *bhakti.*

Bhakti The love felt by the spiritual seeker of Truth towards the Guru or God. The path of devotion. The spiritual attitude of service to the Guru or God which helps purify the mind.

Buddhi Sanskrit term for intellect.

Darshan Blessings by the presence and grace of the Guru or God. Darshan is usually given through sight, touch or by being in the presence of the Guru, physically or non-physically.

Guru An enlightened spiritual teacher or master; the dispeller of darkness and ego; one who helps you dive within and realise the true Self.

Heart Not the physical heart nor the emotional centre, but used as a synonym for the Supreme Self.

Mala A set of beads strung together which have spiritual significance in Hindu and Buddhist traditions. They are either worn as a garland around the neck or are used similarly to the rosary in the Christian tradition to keep count while reciting, chanting or mentally repeating a prayer, a mantra or the various names of God.

Maya The illusion or dream of duality in the phenomenal universe.

Papaji Sri HWL Poonja is a disciple of Sri Ramana Maharshi. He left the earthly realm in 1997. Although considered an Advaita Master, he is not confined to any particular tradition. Papaji is Mooji's Master.

Prasad Blessed food offering.

Ramana Maharshi A Sage widely known for the power of his Self-realisation as well as his devotion and union with the holy mountain of Arunachala in south India. He departed the physical realm in 1950. Sri Ramana recommends self-inquiry as an unsparing tool to erode the persistent habit of identifying with the ego. Mooji's own Master, Papaji, is a direct disciple of Sri Ramana.

Sadhana Ego-transcending spiritual practice, such as meditation.

Samadhi In its highest meaning, this Sanskrit term refers to a state where mind is irretrievably merged in Self-awareness. Even though body consciousness, thoughts and life's activities continue playing, they no longer cause confusion about one's true nature.

Sangha A community of beings who, in following the call of the inner voice of Self-discovery, find themselves drawn towards a particular spiritual master who can guide them to realise the Truth.

Satguru A spiritual preceptor of the highest attainment, one who has realised the ultimate Truth. Also the inner Guru, one's true Self, the impersonal, the Absolute.

Satori Sudden enlightenment and a state of consciousness attained by intuitive illumination.

Satsang Association with the highest Truth. Satsang also refers to meetings where seekers can ask questions and receive guidance from a teacher or master.

Vasanas Deep-rooted habitual tendencies that belong to and re-inforce a personal identity. They carry a strong emotional charge.

Zen Emphasises insight into Buddha nature and imparts that the potential to awaken is inherent in everyone. One awakens not by the study or through rites and ceremonies, but by breaking through the boundaries of mundane logical thought.

Acknowledgements

Mooji's guidance and care has imbued this project
with love, joy and grace. We feel truly blessed
and honoured to be able to participate in the sharing
of our beloved Master's pointings, and are deeply
grateful for the opportunity to be of service in this way.

Design support
Amrita, Florentina, Prabha

Editing support
Darshana, Jorg, Krishnabai, Lakshmi, Samadhi

Transcribing of quotes
Abe, Amala, Bhagavati, Bodhi Ma, Darshana,
Deva, Ganga Ma, Gangotri, GitaSri, Indira, Jaya,
Lucia, Mantra, Mirabai, Nirvani, Nurit, Omkara,
Priya, Samadhi, Satyadevi, Shankar, Shanti,
Soham, Shrimayi, Sahaja Express editors

Photographers
Amrita, Darshana, Gautami Arsénio, Jyoti, Nitya

Special thanks
The irrepressible Mooji Sangha for all your support
and daily acts of love, care and authenticity which
are the evidence of the Truth shining in your Heart.

With love
Mooji Media Publications

(Anthony Paul Moo-Young)

Advaita zen master Mooji is unlike anyone else you are likely to meet, for he compels one to question one's very nature and existence. From the very first encounter, people from all walks of life are deeply touched by his indefinable presence, and perhaps for the very first time experience a natural sense of happiness and peace as they come to discover who or what they truly are.

Mooji was born in Jamaica on 29 January, 1954. As a teenager he moved to London, UK, where he later worked as a street portrait artist and then as an art teacher in the local college. In 1987, an encounter with a Christian mystic inspired Mooji to 'walk out of his life'—an expression he uses to convey the profundity of that meeting. In 1993, Mooji travelled to India, where seemingly by chance, he met his Master, Sri HWL Poonja, or Papaji, as he is affectionately known by his devotees. At Papaji's feet, whatever still remained of an active ego was finally uprooted.

Recognising Mooji's radiance, people from various parts of the world soon began to approach him to simply sit in his presence and to ask questions regarding their search for Truth. The capacity to guide them arose spontaneously in him. While Mooji's presence exudes compassion and devotion, his unity with Truth is also potently shared through self-inquiry—the unsparing light of wisdom which dispels the delusions and suffering common to human experiencing.

In his direct and open interactions, each one who meets Mooji with a genuine urge for freedom is pulled by his profound unconditional love and the power of his pointings into the recognition of the infinite Self we already are. Mooji presently resides at Monte Sahaja in Portugal and he continues to share Satsang worldwide with all who yearn to discover their true nature.

Further details about Mooji's work
and schedule are available at:
www.mooji.org

For Mooji's other books *Vaster Than Sky Greater Than Space,*
The Mala of God, Before I Am (2nd Edition), Writing on Water
and *Breath of the Absolute,* and satsang recordings in audio
and video formats, you are welcome to visit:
www.mooji.org/shop

Video and audio satsang recordings can
also be found on: **www.mooji.tv**

Mooji is also on YouTube: **www.youtube.com/moojiji**
and Facebook: **www.facebook.com/moojiji**

For additional information and enquiries
about books please contact:

Mooji Media Publications

office@moojimedia.com

www.moojimedia.com